taste

Seasonal Dishes
from a Prairie Table

CJ Katz

foreword by ANITA STEWART

University of Regina

CPRC
PRESS
WWW.CPRCPRESS.CA

Printed and bound in Canada at Friesens.
The text of this book is printed on 100% post-consumer recycled paper with earth-friendly vegetable-based inks.

PROJECT EDITOR: Deborah Rush   INDEXER/PROOFREADER: Karen Griffiths
COPY EDITOR: Donna Grant   COVER AND TEXT DESIGN: Duncan Campbell

Photos of CJ ice fishing on Katepwa Lake (page 173) by Gareth Dillistone; photo of durum wheat (page 186) courtesy of Saskatchewan Ministry of Agriculture; photos of honey mushrooms (pages 56 and 57) by Gerry Ivanochko; photos of pastry method (page 86) by Shaq Tcherni. All other photos by CJ Katz.

Library and Archives Canada Cataloguing in Publication

Katz, CJ
Taste : seasonal dishes from a prairie table / CJ Katz; foreword by Anita Stewart.

(Trade books based in scholarship ; 33)
Includes bibliographical references and index.
ISBN 978-0-88977-277-9

1. Cooking, Canadian—Prairie style. 2. Cooking—Prairie Provinces. 3. Cookbooks I. Title. II. Series: TBS ; 33

TX715.6.K38 2012   641.59712   C2012-901902-X

10   9   8   7   6   5   4   3   2   1

CPRC
PRESS

Canadian Plains Research Center Press, University of Regina
Regina, Saskatchewan, Canada, S4S 0A2
tel: (306) 585-4758 fax: (306) 585-4699
e-mail: canadian.plains@uregina.ca web: www.cprcpress.ca

We acknowledge the financial support of the Government of Canada through the Canada Book Fund for our publishing activities, and the Creative Industry Growth and Sustainability program which is made possible through funding provided to the Saskatchewan Arts Board by the Government of Saskatchewan through the Ministry of Tourism, Parks, Culture and Sport.

 Canadian Heritage Patrimoine canadien  Government of Saskatchewan SASKATCHEWAN ARTS BOARD

To the men in my life: my husband Michael,
and my two beautiful sons, Aidan and Benjamin,
who have been steadfast supporters of every project I take on...
and who gladly let me spoil them
with my many culinary creations.

contents

foreword

From the ancient mystery of the Cypress Hills and the windswept grasslands of the south to the meandering, glacial-fed rivers in the heart of the province to the dense, boreal forest and watery north, Saskatchewan is a land of great contrast and extraordinary beauty. When I write that "Canada is food," there are few other regions where this is so obvious. Look on either side of any highway. Over the rolling countryside and duck-dotted sloughs, you'll see thousands of acres of wheat and lentils and canola. There are chickpeas and sky-blue flax and dense berry hedgerows; wild rice and freshwater fish; bison and beef.

No other province in Confederation has such defined borders. And although it's about the same physical size as France, where 63.5 million people put an ever-increasing strain on its 675,000 square kilometres, Saskatchewan has less than 1/60th of that country's population. People are light on the ground here. It follows that the struggle to understand the regional foodways has always been a challenge and, frankly, few have really tried. They were all too busy just surviving...dust storms one year, floods the next, often in concert with financial hardship and low commodity prices. From locusts and forest fires to tornadoes, frosts and blizzards, Saskatchewan has experienced nearly every natural disaster a continental climate has to offer. The history of the province is filled with tenacity and pride and innovation...and lots of church suppers.

Enter CJ Katz...with her camera, her curiosity and her talent as a storyteller. And she's done it! She's explored the province, broadcasting the culinary tales she's uncovered and sharing her knowledge both locally and nationally. She's captured the spirit.

Throughout this book, CJ's food voice is strong and determined and respectful. Her love of Saskatchewan and its resilient people is well laced with pride. She has chronicled the seasons and cooking traditions with great care. She honours farmers and fishers and a research community that is as creative as any.

With *Taste: Seasonal Dishes from a Prairie Table* CJ pays homage to her home and invites us to share a generous, delicious glimpse inside the kitchens and across the expanse of this magnificent province.

—Anita Stewart, CM, author, culinary activist, creator of Food Day Canada

introduction

I am blessed to live in Saskatchewan, the heart of the Canadian Prairies. Saskatchewan has been my family's home province for ten years and we have fallen in love with the land, the people, its foods, and its seasons.

Indeed, the prairie seasons, as well as my experiences of discovering and writing about the foods that grow on the Prairies, have inspired the creation of the recipes in this, my first cookbook, *Taste: Seasonal Dishes from a Prairie Table*. These recipes, many of which were originally presented during the first five years of my cooking show, *The Wheatland Café* on CTV, take advantage of fresh ingredients and celebrate each season's diversity and bounty.

The Spring section features ingredients such as tender fiddleheads, fresh fish, and sweet honey that beckon us when days lengthen and the sun's rays warm the earth. Summer recipes lay out an abundant smorgasbord of earthy mushrooms, prairie lamb, and sweet berries that inspire our culinary imaginations as we shop at farmers' markets. The Autumn section gives thanks for a bountiful harvest with comforting braises and bakings made with wild rice, apples, bison, and pumpkins. While the land sleeps, Winter recipes send us to our pantry and freezer to make lentil and bean soups, hearty meat pies, and cheery holiday desserts that recall the seasons past.

Yet, our connection to the food we eat begins not just with each season, but also with the land and its people. Throughout *Taste*, you will find many photographs that I took while traveling around the province; the photos and the vignettes feature prairie produce and prairie producers—you'll see pike being reeled in on a glorious Saskatchewan lake, pumpkins greeting visitors at a vegetable farm, organic lentils being harvested, tomatoes and hot peppers ready for purchase at an outdoor market, majestic bison grazing, a beekeeper tending her honeybees, and yes, an iconic field of prairie wheat, ripe for harvesting. What a joy it was to travel around the province, meeting so many hard-working producers, and discovering the diversity and richness that is our own backyard.

Now, it's time to turn the page. Fire your spirit. Feed your soul. And taste the bounty of the Prairies.

SPRING MENUS

WEEKEND FAMILY CASUAL GET-TOGETHER

Artichoke Dip with Seeded Crackers **10**

Asparagus Soup **3**

Walleye with Chipotle-Lime Sauce **16**

Fiddleheads with
Easy Lemony Hollandaise Sauce **8**

*Tossed Spring Greens
with Simple Vinaigrette*

Granola Bâtards **44**

Old-Fashioned White Cake **36**

Fresh Berries

WEEKNIGHT MEAL

Asparagus with
Fresh Basil Pesto **9**

Aunt Jean's Honey Chicken
and Scented Rice **25**

Nouveaux Strawberries and Cream **32**

SUNDAY AFTERNOON TEA

Mixed Berry Shortcakes **34**

Orange-Saffron Babycakes **37**

Rhubarb Galette **33**

Honey Spice Cookies **39**

Triple-Chocolate Cookies **40**

Fresh Fruit Cups

Tea and Coffee

SUMMER MENUS

SMOKY BACKYARD BARBEQUE

Curried Vegetable Soup with Orzo,
served in mugs **51**

Spicy Tomato and Cucumber Salad **60**

Smoked Steelhead Trout **76**
or Chili-Rubbed Steelhead Trout **77**

Beer and Molasses Marinated
Flank Steak **73**

Perfect Peach and Blueberry
Lattice Pie **88**

WEEKEND BRUNCH

Roasted Tomato and Vegetable Soup **49**

Sun-Dried Tomato and Ricotta Lasagne **78**

Crunchy Broccoli Salad **60**

Tossed Salad

Cornmeal-Blueberry Muffins **92**

Sour Cherry Pie **89**

Premium Vanilla Ice Cream

CANADA DAY BARBEQUE

Spicy Chipotle Bison Burgers **64**

Rob's Southern Barbeque-Style
Pulled Pork Sandwiches **74**

Oil and Vinegar Coleslaw

Sliced Garden-Fresh Tomatoes

White Chocolate Berry Semifreddo **82**

Dark Chocolate Cherry Brownies **84**

AUTUMN MENUS

THANKSGIVING

Roasted Butternut Squash Soup **99**

Sliced Beets with Warm Chèvre **101**

Roast Turkey with Stuffing

Stuffed Mini Pumpkins **104**

Oven-Roasted Brussels Sprouts

Pumpkin Pie **137**

Apple Dumplings **134**

Vanilla-Scented Whipped Cream

GAME DAY GATHERING

Prairie Antipasto Platter **102**

Chili Con Carne **127**

Tortilla Chips or Buns

Apple Cake with Caramel Glaze **131**

AUTUMN DINNER PARTY

Curried Pumpkin and
Coconut Soup **100**

Pale Ale Braised Pork Belly **128**

Buttermilk Mashed Potatoes

Herb and Garlic Roasted Carrots **112**

Whole Wheat-Quinoa Bread **147**

Apple Wontons **133**

Premium Vanilla Ice Cream

WINTER MENUS

WINE TASTING DINNER PARTY

Smoky Chipotle Hummus **163**

Crisp Pita Chips

Succulent Stuffed Chicken Breasts
with Red Wine Sauce **180**

Sun-Dried Tomato and
Basil Mashed Potatoes **162**

Oven-Roasted Beets

Lingonberry Cheesecake
with Sweet Lingonberry Sauce **190**

TOBOGGAN PARTY

Saskatchewan Soup **154**

Cowboy Beef Pie or Turnovers **166**

Creamy Coleslaw

Bread Pudding with Brandied Fruit **187**

VEGETARIAN BUFFET

Mushroom-Barley Soup **153**

Braised Lentils **160**

Winter Bean Curry **177**

Brown Rice

Squash Bake **160**

Mary's Marinated Beets **163**

Apple-Lingonberry Strudel **184**

Lentil Chocolate Cake **185**

Rugelach **194**

Life stirs beneath the melting snows,

The blustery Prairies awaken,

Warm winds breathe forth new life, longer days,

Canada geese honk their return; new-born lambs bleat their arrival; songbirds mate.

Flowers await the honeybee's dance.

Chive shoots, tart rhubarb, tender asparagus,

Nourishing woodland mushrooms and fronds...

The time of renewal.

The time of blossoming.

My backyard comes alive with apple blossoms every spring.

spring

Asparagus Soup

Asparagus is quintessentially Canadian. It grows everywhere. As I was growing up, each spring my brother John and I would walk along the grassy ditches near our house with our heads bowed and a bag in hand, keeping our eyes peeled for the telltale tall, slender stalks. It was local food at its best. This flavourful, bright green soup showcases the first produce of spring.

SERVES 6

2 lbs (907 g) **fresh asparagus**

8 **green onions**, finely sliced

4 tbsp (60 mL) **unsalted butter**

3 tbsp (45 mL) **unbleached all-purpose flour**

6 cups (1.5 L) **chicken** or vegetable **stock**

$^1/_2$ cup (125 mL) **35% cream**, or half and half

2 tbsp (30 mL) finely chopped **fresh tarragon**, or 2 tsp (10 mL) dried tarragon

1 tbsp (15 mL) **dry** (not cream) **sherry** (optional)

salt and pepper, to taste

Rinse the asparagus to remove any grit. Snap the tough ends off with your hands. The ends will snap off right where the tender and tough parts meet.

Meanwhile, bring a medium pot with salted water to a boil. Add the prepared asparagus and cook, covered, for about 3 to 4 minutes. Drain. Chop into 1-inch (2.5 cm) long pieces, reserving some of the tips for garnish.

In a large pot or Dutch oven, melt the butter over medium heat; add the green onions and season lightly with salt and pepper. Let sweat, covered over very low heat, for several minutes. Do not brown. Add the flour and stir for one minute. Add the chicken stock and the cooked asparagus. Cover and bring to a boil. Simmer about 15 minutes or until the asparagus is very soft.

Using a blender or food processor, purée the mixture in batches and transfer to another pot. Add cream, fresh tarragon, and dry sherry, if using. Season with salt and pepper to taste. Heat through but do not boil.

Ladle into soup bowls and garnish with cooked asparagus tips or a few fresh tarragon leaves.

Asparagus with Morels

The first tastes of spring combine to make a delicious side dish.

SERVES 4

1 tbsp (15 mL) **vegetable oil**

1 tbsp (15 mL) **unsalted butter**

1 tbsp (15 mL) finely chopped **shallots**

1 small or half a large clove **garlic**

¼ cup (60 mL) **dry white wine**

½ cup (125 mL) **35% cream**

3 oz (85 g) **fresh morels**, or ½ oz (14 g) dried (see sidebar)

1 lb (454 g) **fresh asparagus**

salt and **pepper**, to taste

In a pan over medium-low heat, add the oil and butter. Melt until bubbly. Add the shallots and garlic, and sauté for 1 minute.

Add the white wine and reduce by half. (If using dried mushrooms, also add the reserved mushroom liquid and let the mixture simmer until the liquid has reduced by half).

Add the cream and morels and cover with a lid. Let simmer about 3 to 5 minutes. Remove lid and continue to simmer until the cream has thickened. Season with salt and a pinch of pepper.

Meanwhile, rinse the asparagus to remove any grit. Snap the tough ends off with your hands. The ends will snap off right where the tender and tough parts meet. Steam the asparagus spears until tender crisp.

Place the cooked asparagus on a serving plate. Top with the morel sauce. Serve warm.

Using Fresh and Dried Morels

If using fresh morels, rinse them well to remove any grit and sand. Leave small ones whole and halve the large ones.

If using dried morels, set the morels in a dish and add about 1 cup (250 mL) boiling water. Cover the dish with a plate and let stand about 1 hour. Swish the morels with your hands to remove any grit and dirt, and then rinse them under running water. Set a coffee filter over a glass and pour the liquid from the soaked mushrooms into the filter to drain and capture any grit. Reserve the liquid and use as described in the recipe.

Asparagus and Fiddlehead Quinoa Salad

Fiddleheads and asparagus are among the first greens of spring. To keep fiddleheads fresh, put them into a bowl, cover them with cold water, and store them in the coldest part of your fridge. They will last for weeks. If you can't find fiddleheads for this recipe, just add more asparagus or green beans for a nutritious salad.

SERVES 6

1 cup (250 mL) **quinoa**

2 cups (500 mL) **water**

1 cup (250 mL) trimmed **asparagus**, cut into 1-inch (2.5 cm) pieces

2 cups (500 mL) **fresh fiddleheads**

1 cup (250 mL) diced and seeded **English cucumber**

3/4 cup (185 mL) sliced **cherry tomatoes**

2/3 cup (160 mL) diced **red pepper**

1/4 cup (60 mL) *each* chopped **fresh tarragon**, chopped **fresh chives**, and chopped **fresh parsley**

5 to 6 tbsp (75 to 90 mL) **fresh lemon juice**

5 tbsp (75 mL) **extra virgin olive oil**

1/2 tsp (2 mL) **Dijon mustard**

1/2 tsp (2 mL) **kosher salt**

1/4 tsp (1 mL) freshly ground **black pepper**

Place the quinoa in a sieve and rinse under cold water for 3 minutes to remove any bitterness from the outer husk. In a medium-sized pot with a lid, bring the water to a boil. Reduce the heat and add the quinoa. Cook, covered, for about 20 to 25 minutes. Remove the lid and fluff the quinoa with a fork. Let stand, uncovered, about 10 minutes; then spread on a parchment paper-lined cookie sheet, and let sit until cool.

Bring a pot with 4 cups (1 L) water to a boil. Add 1 tsp (5 mL) salt. Cook the asparagus for 2 minutes. Remove with a slotted spoon into an ice-water bath to cool quickly.

Add the fiddleheads into the same boiling water and cook for 2 minutes. Remove with a slotted spoon and put them into the same ice-water bath. When the asparagus and fiddleheads are completely cool, drain the vegetables, and dry them with a towel.

In a large bowl, combine the cooled quinoa, cooled asparagus and fiddleheads, cucumber, cherry tomatoes, red pepper, fresh tarragon, chives, and parsley. Toss gently.

In a small bowl, whisk together the lemon juice, olive oil, Dijon mustard, salt, and pepper. Pour over the salad and toss gently to combine. Taste, and add more lemon juice, salt, and pepper, if desired.

fiddleheads
EARLY FOREST GEMS

There have been songs and poetry written about fiddleheads. And why not? Their short season keeps us pining, like long-distance lovers who embrace but once a year. We yearn for a big feed as the snow begins to melt and the brooks begin to flow. Is it because we've survived yet another frigid winter? Is our body craving a vitamin and mineral boost? Perhaps we simply adore their slightly bitter asparagus and artichoke flavour.

These spring delicacies are the tiny, bright green, unfurled fronds of the fern. The most commonly picked variety is the ostrich fern. Fiddleheads, which are not grown commercially in Saskatchewan, are plucked from the woods from mid-May through early June. You'll find them popping up in damp, shady forest areas all over Canada, particularly in the Maritimes and southeastern Quebec. The most productive regions in Saskatchewan are around Carrot River, Nipawin, White Fox, and the Cumberland House Delta.

Fiddleheads should always be eaten cooked. Fresh-picked raw fiddleheads can be covered with cold water and stored in the coldest part of your fridge for weeks. For longer storage, blanche them for two minutes and freeze them in zip-lock bags. I love these high-antioxidant greens prepared very simply with a drizzle of olive oil, a sprinkle of coarse salt, and just a squirt of lemon. For a change of pace, purée them into a bright green cream soup, or marinate them and toss some into a salad. They're delicious combined with another early forest gem: the morel.

Freshly picked fiddleheads from northern Saskatchewan.

Fiddleheads with Easy Lemony Hollandaise Sauce

Fiddleheads are adored by many Canadians, who wait eagerly for this delicacy as soon as the snow melts and the earth begins to warm. The fiddlehead season is extremely short, so we tend to eat them at practically every meal until they are no longer available. The hollandaise sauce is a recipe from my childhood. It's delicious on just about any green vegetable. I especially love it with fiddleheads and asparagus.

SERVES 4 TO 6

3 to 4 cups (750 mL to 1 L) **fresh fiddleheads**, cleaned and trimmed

HOLLANDAISE SAUCE

3 **egg yolks**

2 tbsp (30 mL) **fresh lemon juice**

2 to 3 sprigs **fresh parsley**

One 3/8-inch (1 cm) thick **onion** slice

1/2 tsp (2 mL) **kosher salt**

1/8 tsp (.5 mL) **pepper**

1/2 cup (125 mL) **unsalted butter,** room temperature

1/2 cup (125 mL) **boiling water**

Fill the bottom of a double boiler* about half full with water. Bring to a boil, then reduce to a simmer. The top of the double boiler should sit *over* but not *in* the simmering water.

Meanwhile, in a blender or food processor, combine the egg yolks, lemon juice, parsley, onion, salt, pepper, and butter. Blend until smooth, about 5 seconds. With the motor running, gradually add 1/2 cup (125 mL) boiling water.

Pour the mixture into the top of the double boiler. Cook the sauce, whisking briskly until it is the consistency of soft custard. Immediately remove the top portion or bowl from the heat and keep the sauce warm. Do not discard the water from the pot.

Bring the hot water in the pot back to a boil. Add a pinch of salt and the fiddleheads. Cook 2 to 3 minutes. Drain.

Serve the cooked fiddleheads with the sauce.

** If you do not have a double boiler, use a medium pot and a medium-sized metal bowl. The bowl should sit **over** but not **in** the simmering water in the pot.*

Asparagus with Fresh Basil Pesto

The combination of basil and asparagus is a "match made in heaven." Forget buying pesto. It's a snap to make and supermarket brands don't stand a chance against the flavour of freshly made pesto right from your own backyard or a farmers' market. Use Parmesan cheese sold in a block, not the canned or pre-shredded variety.

SERVES 4

1 lb (454 g) **fresh asparagus**

extra virgin olive oil, for drizzling

kosher salt, for sprinkling

several spoonfuls **Fresh Basil Pesto**

fresh Parmesan cheese

Preheat barbeque to high.

Rinse the asparagus to remove any grit. Snap the tough ends off with your hands. The ends will snap off right where the tender and tough parts meet. Place the spears in a shallow dish and drizzle with olive oil and sprinkle liberally with salt. Toss to coat well.

Reduce heat to medium. Place asparagus in a grill basket and grill with the lid down for about 10 minutes, turning regularly, until the asparagus is slightly charred but still tender crisp. While the asparagus is grilling, make the pesto. (NOTE: The recipe below will be more than you require.)

To serve the grilled asparagus, toss with several spoonfuls of Fresh Basil Pesto. Top with a few shavings of fresh Parmesan cheese. Serve warm or at room temperature.

Fresh Basil Pesto

MAKES ABOUT 1 1/2 CUPS

2 handfuls **fresh basil leaves**

2 to 3 cloves **garlic**, peeled

1/4 cup (60 mL) toasted **pine nuts**

1 to 2 oz (28 to 56 g) **Parmesan cheese** (broken up or coarsely grated)

1 tsp or more (5 mL or more) **red wine vinegar**, to taste

about 1 cup (250 mL) **extra virgin olive oil**

kosher salt, to taste

In a food processor bowl, combine the basil leaves, garlic, pine nuts, Parmesan cheese, 1 tsp (5 mL) red wine vinegar, and about 1/2 cup (125 mL) olive oil. Process until fairly fine. Add more olive oil, as needed, until a paste forms; it should be more wet than dry. Taste and adjust seasonings, adding salt and up to 1 tsp (5 mL) more red wine vinegar.

Transfer any unused pesto to a jar. To store the pesto, cover the paste with about 1/8 inch (3 mm) additional olive oil to prevent air from reaching the pesto. Pesto can be kept for several weeks in the refrigerator.

Basil Pesto

Pesto is delicious as a flavouring for scrambled eggs, as a marinade for chicken, brushed on cooked fish, or thinned with additional olive oil and used as a salad dressing.

Artichoke Dip with Seeded Crackers

Summers on the prairies burst with locally-grown produce. In this tasty recipe, the fresh flavours of green onions, red pepper, and pungent basil join with artichokes to create an irresistible combination. The crispy crackers add a delicious contrast to the creaminess of the dip.

MAKES 2 CUPS (500 ML)

Artichoke Dip

14 oz (398 mL) **artichokes**, canned in water (not oil)

2 **green onions**, very thinly sliced

2 to 3 tbsp (30 to 45 mL) **red pepper**, finely diced

1/4 cup (60 mL) **plain yogurt**

1/4 cup (60 mL) **mayonnaise**

1 tbsp (15 mL) finely sliced **fresh basil**

1/2 cup (125 mL) finely shredded **fresh Parmesan cheese**

1/4 tsp (1 mL) freshly ground **black pepper**

pinch **kosher salt**

Drain the artichokes and rinse with water. Finely chop them with a knife.

In a medium bowl, combine the artichokes with the green onions, red pepper, yogurt, mayonnaise, fresh basil, Parmesan cheese, black pepper, and a pinch of salt.

Taste and adjust seasonings. Refrigerate until ready to serve. Can be made a day ahead.

Millet grown at Daybreak-Scheresky farm, Estevan.

Seeded Crackers

1 package (1 lb/454 g) **egg roll wrappers**

1 **egg white**, for brushing

1 tbsp (15 mL) **water**

1 tbsp (15 mL) **fleur de sel** or other finishing salt

1 tbsp (15 mL) **poppy seeds**

1 tbsp (15 mL) **anise seeds**

1 tbsp (15 mL) **millet** or sesame seeds

Preheat oven to 350°F (180°C).

Line a cookie sheet with parchment paper. In a small bowl, beat the egg white with a fork together with 1 tbsp (15 mL) water until foamy.

In another small bowl, combine the poppy seeds, anise seeds and millet seeds. Set aside.

Lay three or four egg roll wrappers on a clean surface. Brush both sides of each wrapper with the beaten egg white. Sprinkle one side with fleur de sel and some of the seed mixture.

With a sharp knife or pizza cutter, slice each sheet diagonally to form four triangles. Place each triangle seeded side up on the parchment paper–lined cookie sheet, leaving space between each triangle.

Bake for 6 to 8 minutes, until the edges start to brown and small bubbles appear all over the cracker. Remove from the oven and transfer the crackers to a wire rack. Crackers will get crispy as they cool.

Repeat the procedure until you have the desired number of crackers. (NOTE: The package will have more egg roll wrappers than you will require.) Crackers can be made several days ahead and stored in an airtight container.

Gravad Steelhead Trout with Dill-Cream Sauce

When I was in my early twenties, I spent four years in Sweden and fell in love with Gravad Lax, a salt-and-sugar-cured fish dish traditionally made with salmon. My version, made with Lake Diefenbaker steelhead trout, is served with a non-traditional dill-cream sauce taught to me by a Swedish chef.

SERVES 4

Fresh dill in bloom.

1 **fresh Lake Diefenbaker trout fillet**, skin-on, about 1 to 1 1/2 lbs (454 to 680 g)

1/2 tbsp (7 mL) coarsely crushed **black peppercorns**

1 1/2 tbsp (22 mL) **granulated sugar**

3/4 tbsp (10 mL) **fleur de sel**, or coarse salt

2 bunches **dill**, finely chopped, about 4 tbsp (60 mL) (divided)

cucumber slices, **lemon slices** and extra **dill**, for garnish

Lay the fillet, skin side down, on a cutting board. Run your fingers along the flesh to feel for bones and use a pair of tweezers to remove them. Wash the fish and pat it dry with a paper towel. Cut the fillet in half crosswise.

In a small bowl, combine the pepper, sugar, and salt. Set aside.

In a rectangular glass or ceramic dish large enough to fit the halved trout fillet, sprinkle 1/3 of the salt mixture on the bottom of the dish and then sprinkle with 1/4 of the chopped dill. Place the wider fillet, skin side down and flesh side up, on the salt mixture. Sprinkle the top of fillet with 1/3 of the salt mixture and then with 1/4 of the dill. Place the second fillet, flesh side down and skin side up, on top of first fillet, and sprinkle with the remaining salt mixture and 1/4 of the dill. (Reserve the remaining dill for sauce.)

Cover the prepared fish with plastic wrap and then cover with tea towel. Rest one or two bricks or a cast-iron fry pan on top of the tea towel to press down the fillets (do not skip this step). Refrigerate for a minimum of 24 hours, preferably 48 to 72 hours. Turn the fillets over half way through the marinating process. Each day, pour off the liquid as it accumulates.

When the fish is fully cured, use a long sharp knife to slice each fillet on a diagonal into very thin slices, cutting each slice away from the skin.

Serve with the Dill-Cream Sauce and garnish each serving with thinly sliced cucumber, lemon slices, and sprigs of fresh dill.

Dill-Cream Sauce

1/2 cup (125 mL) **35% cream**

1/2 cup (125 mL) **mayonnaise**

1 tbsp (15 mL) finely chopped **fresh dill**

pinch **kosher salt**

Whip the cream to very stiff peaks. Using a spatula, very gently fold the mayonnaise into the whipped cream (do not use the mixer or the sauce will deflate). Fold in the dill. Add a pinch of salt. Taste and adjust seasonings.

Warm Walleye Salad with Basil Mayo

This light salad is great as a lunch or supper option.

SERVES 2

1 boneless, skinless **walleye fillet** or **bass fillet**

1 **egg**

1 cup (250 mL) **milk**

¼ cup (60 mL) **cornmeal**

¼ cup (60 mL) **unbleached all-purpose flour**

¼ cup (60 mL) **rice flour** or cornstarch

½ tsp (2 mL) **garlic powder**

½ tsp (2 mL) **black pepper**

1 tsp (5 mL) **kosher salt**

1 tsp (5 mL) **dried thyme**

1 tsp (5 mL) **paprika powder**

vegetable oil, for frying

3 to 4 cups (750 mL to 1 L) **mixed greens**

1 to 2 medium **tomatoes**, sliced

⅓ of an **English cucumber**, sliced

several thin slices **red onion**

any other vegetables you like in your salad

Walleye

There is plenty of confusion about the correct name for walleye; people often refer to it as pickerel. Diehard Saskatchewan anglers will quickly correct you. Indeed, the fish are unrelated, with walleye coming from the *Percidae* family, and pickerel coming from the *Esocidae* family.

In a medium bowl, whisk together the egg and the milk.

In a small bowl, combine the cornmeal, unbleached all-purpose flour, rice flour or cornstarch, garlic powder, black pepper, kosher salt, dried thyme, and paprika powder. Mix together, and transfer to a disposable plastic bag.

Rinse the fish and pat dry with a paper towel. Cut the fillet lengthwise down the middle to separate it into two long strips. Cut each strip crosswise in half.

Dip each piece of fish into the egg-milk mixture, then into the cornmeal-flour mixture to coat completely. Set aside on a plate.

Heat a grill pan on medium heat. Add oil. Fry the fish pieces until just cooked through, about 5 minutes per side. Set aside on paper towel to drain for several minutes.

On two individual dinner plates, place a mound of the mixed greens. Top with sliced tomatoes, sliced cucumber, sliced red onion, and any other vegetables you prefer. Place two pieces of warm fish on top of the salad.

Garnish the fish with a dollop of the Basil Mayo.

Basil Mayo

¼ cup (60 mL) **mayonnaise**

¼ cup (60 mL) **plain yogurt**

2 tbsp (30 mL) finely chopped **fresh basil**

½ tsp (2 mL) **Dijon mustard**

kosher salt, to taste

In a medium bowl, whisk together the mayonnaise, yogurt, fresh basil, Dijon mustard, and salt. Cover and refrigerate until ready to serve.

13

Grilled Chicken Salad

The fresh flavour of basil is like Saskatchewan sunshine, bright and uplifting. Enjoy this marinated chicken on its own or with the mixed baby greens as suggested here for a satisfying main dish summer salad.

SERVES 6 AS A MAIN DISH

6 boneless, skinless **chicken breasts**

8 to 10 cups (2 to 2.5 L) **mesclun** or baby salad greens

PESTO

1 large handful **fresh basil leaves**, without stems

2 small **Thai red chili peppers**, or 1 seeded jalapeño pepper

2 cloves **garlic**, peeled

$^{1}/_{3}$ cup (80 mL) toasted **pine nuts**

1 tsp (5 mL) grated **fresh ginger**

4 to 5 sprigs **fresh cilantro**

1 tbsp (15 mL) **brown sugar**

$^{1}/_{2}$ tsp (2 mL) **kosher salt**

$^{1}/_{4}$ tsp (1 mL) freshly ground **black pepper**

about $^{1}/_{2}$ cup (125 mL) **extra virgin olive oil**

LIME VINAIGRETTE

2 tbsp (30 mL) **fresh lime juice**

4 to 6 tbsp (60 to 90 mL) **extra virgin olive oil**

1 tsp (5 mL) **Dijon mustard**

salt and **pepper**, to taste

PESTO: To make the pesto, combine the fresh basil leaves, chili peppers, garlic cloves, pine nuts, ginger, cilantro, brown sugar, salt, and pepper in a food processor bowl. Pulse until coarsely chopped. With motor running, add olive oil, and process until a coarse paste forms.

Place chicken breasts and pesto in a zip-lock plastic bag. Seal the bag and toss to coat the chicken breasts. Refrigerate several hours or overnight.

Preheat barbeque.* Grill the chicken breasts until cooked through, about 7 minutes per side depending on their thickness. Remove from the grill. Drape with a sheet of waxed paper and cover with a tea towel. Let rest 10 minutes.

LIME VINAIGRETTE: In a small bowl, whisk together the fresh lime juice and olive oil. Whisk in the Dijon mustard, salt, and pepper. Toss with the salad greens.

To serve, slice the chicken breasts on the diagonal. Place a mound of dressed greens on a plate and top with the sliced chicken breast.

The chicken breasts can also be cooked in a stove-top grill pan, heated to medium-high.

Walleye with Chipotle-Lime Sauce

People come from great distances to fish for Saskatchewan walleye, a fantastic fish with a delicate, clean flavour. This recipe, with its lightly seasoned breading and a smoked chipotle sauce with a hint of lime, is also terrific made with bass.

SERVES 4 TO 6

Fishing for walleye on the shore of the North Saskatchewan River, Prince Albert, SK.

2 lbs (907 g) boneless, skinless **walleye** or bass **fillets**

1/2 cup (125 mL) **cornstarch**

1 cup (250 ml) **unbleached all-purpose flour**

1/4 cup (60 mL) **cornmeal**

3 tsp (15 mL) **kosher salt**

1 tsp (5 mL) **pepper**

1 tsp (5 mL) **chili powder**

1/2 tsp (2 mL) **garlic powder**

1/2 tsp (2 mL) **onion powder**

1 tsp (5 mL) **dried thyme**

1 **egg**

1 1/2 cups (375 mL) **milk**

vegetable oil, for frying

Rinse the fish and pat dry with a paper towel. Cut the fillets lengthwise down the middle to separate them into two long strips. Cut each strip crosswise into three equal pieces, about 3 to 4 inches (7.5 to 10 cm) long. Cover and refrigerate until ready to cook.

In a medium bowl or plastic zip-lock bag, combine the cornstarch, flour, cornmeal, salt, pepper, chili powder, garlic powder, onion powder, and dried thyme. Mix well and set aside.

In a medium bowl, whisk together the egg and the milk.

Preheat a grill pan or skillet on medium-high heat. Add several tablespoons of oil. Dip the walleye strips into the egg-milk mixture. Using tongs, remove the individual fillets. Toss them in the cornstarch mixture and coat well. Place the coated fish pieces into the hot pan and cook, turning once, about 5 minutes per side, until golden brown. Remove to a paper towel to drain. Serve warm with the Chipotle-Lime Sauce.

Chipotle-Lime Sauce

1/2 cup (125 mL) **plain thick yogurt**

1/2 cup (125 mL) **mayonnaise**

half a **chipotle pepper** canned in adobo sauce, very finely chopped

1 tsp (5 mL) **adobo sauce** from the chipotles, or to taste (optional)

1 **green onion**, very finely sliced

1 **lime**, cut in half

To make the sauce, stir together the thick yogurt, mayonnaise, chipotle pepper, adobo sauce, and green onion. Squeeze a little lime juice into the sauce. Taste and add more lime juice, if desired.

Northern Pike, Last Mountain Lake, SK.

fresh fish
FABULOUS IN EVERY SEASON

Saskatchewan is home to 94,000 lakes and thousands of kilometres of rivers and streams. More than half—50,000 actually—are fish-bearing, and these cover one-eighth of the province, from the grand lakes in the remote north to the smaller lakes and streams in the south. They teem with sixty-nine species of fish: fifty-eight are native species, and one-third are sport fish. Indeed, well over 160,000 fishing licenses are sold each year in the province, one-quarter of which are taken out by non-residents lured with tackle and bait to fly and angle. Sport fishing ranks as the number two attraction behind gaming—and ahead of hunting and our beloved Saskatchewan Roughriders.

While sport fishing in spring through fall is popular, so is winter angling. Even Saskatchewan's frigid winters don't deter the avid fisherman. Many frozen lakes in December through March are dotted with pickup trucks and fishing shacks. In the deep cold, under the wide-open blue sky and glorious sunshine, diehard anglers, well dressed for the occasion, drill through thick ice to "jig" for perch, walleye, pike, whitefish, and trout.

And what is the favoured fish? Saskatchewan walleye is overwhelmingly the preferred fish of the majority of Saskatchewanians and visitors. The white meat is sweet and moist, delicate in flavour, and contains very few bones. It is my favourite Saskatchewan fish. Grilled, poached, or deep-fried...it's fabulous.

Northern pike, also known as jack or jackfish, is highly sought-after and often preferred over walleye. Its flesh is tender and flaky. For the best flavour, fish for pike in very cold water. Correct filleting is essential because the fillets can contain unpleasant Y-shaped bones.

Other popular fish are lake trout, whitefish, perch, Arctic grayling, rainbow trout, and brook trout. Fishing in Saskatchewan is open any time of the year except for a rest period of about four weeks in the spring.

Summer or winter, fishing in the outdoors of Saskatchewan is a Zen-like experience that will leave you refreshed and with a new and unique connection to your food. So...get out and cast your rod!

Steelhead Trout with Asparagus and Papaya

This is a lovely and light spring dish that showcases local asparagus and superb steelhead trout. The vinaigrette has a dual purpose: to marinate the trout and to dress the asparagus and papaya.

SERVES 6

6 **steelhead trout** or salmon **fillets**, skin-on, each 2 inches (5 cm) wide

1/2 cup (125 mL) **olive oil**

1/3 cup (80 mL) **fresh lime juice**

1 **Thai red chili pepper**, finely chopped, or half a seeded jalapeño, finely chopped

finely grated **rind of half a lime**, or more, if desired

pinch **salt** and **pepper**, to taste

1 lb (454 g) **fresh asparagus**

half a **papaya**, peeled and seeded, or 1 mango, peeled

4 **green onions**, finely sliced

2 tbsp (30 mL) coarsely chopped **fresh cilantro**

1/4 cup (60 mL) toasted **pine nuts**

vegetable oil, for grilling

Rinse the fish and pat dry with a paper towel.

To make the vinaigrette, in a small bowl whisk together the olive oil, lime juice, chili pepper, lime rind, salt, and pepper. Pour half over the fillets; reserve the remainder to dress the salad. Refrigerate the fillets for at least 30 minutes but not more than 1 hour.

Preheat barbeque grill or indoor grill pan. Remove the fillets from the vinaigrette. Discard the remaining liquid. Place the fillets skin side up and flesh side down on an oiled hot grill or lightly oiled grill pan. Grill for about 3 to 5 minutes. Turn the fillets and grill another 3 to 5 minutes or until just cooked through.

Meanwhile, snap the bottom end off each asparagus spear. Bring a skillet half full with lightly salted water to a boil. Add the asparagus and cook until tender crisp, about 3 minutes. Drain and set aside.

Dice the papaya or mango. Transfer to a medium bowl. Add the reserved vinaigrette, green onions, cilantro, and toasted pine nuts. Add the warm asparagus spears. Toss gently to coat.

To serve: place one trout fillet on each plate. Top with the asparagus-papaya mixture and add more dressing, if desired.

Spice-Rubbed Walleye with Easy Garlic Aioli

If you like big flavours, this is the dish for you. This recipe is also delicious with other oily-type, white-fleshed fish.

SERVES 4 TO 6

2 lbs (907 g) **boneless, skinless walleye** or bass **fillets**

vegetable oil, for brushing

SPICE RUB

1 tbsp (15 mL) packed **brown sugar**

1 tbsp (15 mL) **dried basil leaves**

1 tbsp (15 mL) **chili powder**

2 tsp (10 mL) freshly ground **black pepper**

1 tsp (5 mL) **smoked paprika**, or sweet paprika

1 tsp (5 mL) **onion powder**

1 tsp (5 mL) **dry mustard**

To make the spice rub, in a small bowl combine the brown sugar, basil leaves, chili powder, black pepper, paprika, onion powder, and dry mustard. Mix well and set aside.

Rinse the fish and pat dry with a paper towel. Brush the fillets with oil. Coat liberally with the spice rub.

Preheat barbeque, or a grill pan for stove-top cooking. Grill or fry the fillets on all sides until cooked through, about 8 to 10 minutes per inch (2.5 cm) of thickness.

Serve the cooked fish topped with a dollop of Easy Garlic Aioli.

Easy Garlic Aioli

4 cloves **garlic**

3/4 cup (185 mL) **mayonnaise**

1 tsp (5 mL) **Dijon mustard**

1 tsp (5 mL) freshly squeezed **lemon juice**

Wrap 4 unpeeled cloves of garlic in foil and bake in a 400°F (200°C) oven for about 30 minutes. During the roasting process, the garlic becomes very soft, slightly sweet, and loses its pungent flavour and aroma. To remove the cloves, squeeze each roasted clove out of its peel with your fingers.

Mash the roasted garlic cloves using a mortar and pestle, or in a small bowl using the back of a spoon. Stir in the mayonnaise, Dijon mustard, and lemon juice. Taste and adjust seasonings. Cover and refrigerate until ready to serve.

Lamb Meatball Wraps

These wraps are stuffed with small meatballs infused with Mediterranean flavours of oregano, mint, cinnamon and lemon, a fresh salad, and a smoky yogurt dressing.

SERVES 4 TO 6—MAKES ABOUT 35 MEATBALLS

LAMB MEATBALLS

1 1/2 lbs (680 g) **ground lamb**

1/2 cup (125 mL) finely chopped **onion**

1/3 cup (80 mL) chopped **fresh mint**

1 tbsp (15 mL) finely chopped **fresh parsley**

1 tsp (5 mL) *each* **dried oregano, ground cumin**, and **ground cinnamon**

1 clove **garlic**, minced

finely grated **rind of 1 lemon**

1 tsp (5 mL) *each* **salt** and **pepper**

SALAD

1 cup (250 mL) **English cucumber**, deseeded and julienned

1 cup (250 mL) finely julienned **carrot**

1 cup (250 mL) finely sliced **red cabbage**

1 clove **garlic**, minced

2 **green onions**, finely sliced

1 tbsp (15 mL) finely chopped **fresh mint**

1 tsp (5 mL) finely chopped **jalapeño**

SMOKY YOGURT DRESSING

1 cup (250 mL) **plain yogurt**

1 tsp (5 mL) **smoked paprika**

1 tsp (5 mL) **ground cumin**

pinch **salt** and **pepper**

1 large **tomato**, halved, and sliced

6 large **soft tortillas**

LAMB MEATBALLS: In a large bowl, mix together the ground lamb, onion, fresh mint, fresh parsley, oregano, cumin, cinnamon, garlic, lemon rind, salt, and pepper. Form into 1 1/4-inch (3 cm) balls. In a preheated skillet over medium-high heat, fry the meatballs in batches until golden brown and cooked through. Remove and drain on a paper towel. Keep warm.

SALAD: In a medium bowl, combine the cucumber, carrots, cabbage, garlic, green onions, mint, and jalapeño. Refrigerate until ready to serve.

SMOKY YOGURT DRESSING: In a small bowl, whisk together the yogurt, smoked paprika, ground cumin, salt, and pepper. Refrigerate until ready to serve.

ASSEMBLY: To make each wrap, lay a tortilla on a flat surface. Place a large handful of the salad down the centre of the tortilla. Top the salad with two or three slices of tomato. Top with five or six meatballs, then several spoonfuls of the dressing. Fold over the sides of the tortilla and place seam-side down on a serving plate.

Chicken with Rosemary-Rhubarb Chutney

Zippy, spice-rubbed chicken pairs beautifully with my Rosemary-Rhubarb Chutney. This dish is great for a backyard barbeque.

SERVES 4

4 boneless, skinless **chicken breasts**

SPICE RUB

1 tbsp (15 mL) **chili powder**

1 tbsp (15 mL) **granulated sugar**

1 tbsp (15 mL) **dried thyme**

1 tbsp (15 mL) freshly ground **black pepper**

1 tsp (5 mL) **garlic powder**

To make the spice rub, in a small bowl, combine the chili powder, sugar, dried thyme, black pepper, and garlic powder. Rub all over the chicken breasts. (Chicken can be prepared to this point and refrigerated until ready to barbeque.)

Preheat barbeque or stove-top grill pan. Cook the chicken breasts over medium heat until no traces of pink remain. Serve with the Rosemary-Rhubarb Chutney.

Rosemary-Rhubarb Chutney

MAKES ABOUT 4 CUPS (1 L)

1 ½ lbs (680 g) **fresh rhubarb**, cut into ¾-inch (2 cm) pieces (about 6 cups), divided

2 cloves **garlic**, minced

half a **red** or white **onion**, sliced into thin wedges

1 to 2 **Thai red chili peppers**, chopped, or 1 jalapeño pepper, seeded and chopped

¾ cup (185 mL) **brown sugar**

¼ cup (60 mL) **malt** or cider **vinegar**

¼ cup (60 mL) **dry red wine**

1 sprig **fresh rosemary**, finely chopped

salt and **pepper**, to taste

In a saucepan, combine 5 cups (1.25 L) rhubarb with the garlic, onion, chili peppers, brown sugar, vinegar, red wine, and fresh rosemary. Bring to a boil. Reduce the heat and simmer about 5 minutes.

Add remaining 1 cup (250 mL) rhubarb and simmer an additional 5 to 10 minutes, until the mixture is slightly thickened but the rhubarb still chunky. Season with salt and pepper. Cool to room temperature and refrigerate until ready to serve.

Aunt Jean's Honey Chicken

This recipe has been in my family for at least five generations, passed down from my paternal grandmother's aunt. It's a favourite of young and old alike.

SERVES 4 TO 6

1 whole **chicken**, about 2 1/2 lbs (1.1 kg), cut up, skin on

1/2 cup (125 mL) **liquid honey**

1/4 cup (60 mL) **unsalted butter**

2 tsp (10 mL) **curry powder**, or Indian-style curry paste

1/4 tsp (1 mL) **dry mustard powder**

pinch **kosher salt**

Preheat oven to 375°F (190°C).

Place chicken pieces in a greased, ovenproof 9- × 13-inch (3.5 L) baking pan.

In a glass measuring cup, combine the honey, butter, curry powder, mustard powder, and salt. Microwave on high for about 1 1/2 minutes. (Alternatively, combine ingredients in a saucepan and heat on the stove until the butter has melted.) Stir well.

Pour the sauce over the chicken pieces and bake, uncovered, for about 40 minutes, basting occasionally. Serve with Scented Rice (recipe on page 120) and a green vegetable.

Herb Roasted Chicken

This tasty roast chicken has a fragrant herbal paste slipped between the meat and the skin to infuse the bird with loads of flavour.

SERVES 6

1 whole **broiler chicken**, about 2 ½ lbs (1.1 kg)

1 tbsp (15 mL) **Dijon mustard**

1 tbsp (15 mL) **liquid honey**

2 tsp (10 mL) chopped **fresh rosemary**

2 tbsp (30 mL) chopped **fresh thyme**

4 **sage leaves**, finely chopped

1 clove **garlic**, peeled and minced

juice of half a lemon

salt and **pepper**

olive oil, for drizzling

1 **onion**, sliced

Preheat oven to 425°F (220°C).

Wash the chicken and pat it dry with paper towel. With your fingers, separate the skin from the flesh across the breast, legs, and thighs, being careful not to tear or puncture the skin.

In a small bowl, combine the mustard, honey, rosemary, thyme, sage, and garlic. Add lemon juice to make a paste.

Using a small spoon, slip the paste between the skin and the flesh on the breast, legs and thighs. Use your fingers to distribute the paste evenly under the skin. Any remaining paste can be "painted" inside the cavity of the chicken with a pastry brush. Sprinkle the inside of the chicken with salt and pepper. Drizzle the outside with olive oil and use your hands to completely coat the bird with the oil. Sprinkle with salt and pepper. Tie the legs closed with butcher twine.

Line the bottom of a shallow, greased pan with the onion slices. Place the chicken breast-side down on top of the onions. Place in the oven and immediately reduce the heat to 325°F (165°C). Roast, uncovered, basting occasionally, for 45 minutes. Remove the chicken from the oven and turn it over. Return to the oven and continue roasting another 15 to 20 minutes, until the chicken is cooked and juices run clear.

Remove the chicken to a platter. Drape with a sheet of waxed paper and then a tea towel. Let rest 15 to 30 minutes. Carve and serve.

Laying hens at the Dodd family farm, Lumsden, SK.

27

Korean Flank Steak

I love flank steak. It's low in price, low in fat, and big on flavour. Most butcher shops carry it, especially during the summer when barbequing is going full tilt in nearly every backyard across the country. A tough cut, it becomes surprisingly tender when sliced very thinly on the diagonal across the grain.

SERVES 4 TO 6

2 lbs (907 g) **flank steak**, trimmed

MARINADE

4 cloves **garlic**, chopped

1 tbsp (15 mL) grated **fresh ginger**

1 small **onion**, sliced into thin wedges

¹⁄₂ cup (125 mL) **soy sauce**

1 tbsp (15 mL) **sesame oil**

2 tbsp (30 mL) **liquid honey**

1 tsp (5 mL) **chili flakes**

To make the marinade, combine the garlic, ginger, onion, soy sauce, sesame oil, honey, and chili flakes in a medium bowl. Place the whole flank steak in a large zip-lock bag and add the marinade. Seal and toss to coat the steak. Refrigerate 4 to 6 hours, or overnight.

Preheat barbeque. Grill steak to medium rare, about 5 to 7 minutes per side, turning once.

Remove to a plate. Drape with a sheet of waxed paper and cover with a tea towel. Let rest 10 minutes. Using a long slicing knife, slice the steak thinly on the diagonal across the grain. Serve warm or at room temperature.

Pizza Dough

Canada has the best flour in the world. Protein levels in Canadian wheat range between 12% and 15%, making it ideal for bread, pasta, and pizza. This pizza dough is excellent when baked on a pizza stone in a very hot oven. Pizza stones are inexpensive and easy to find in most large grocery stores. Often, I will bake a large batch of pizzas and freeze them in individual plastic bags for my sons, Aidan and Benjamin, to take in their lunches. Unused uncooked dough can be frozen in individual portions for later use.

MAKES 18 7-INCH (18 CM) PIZZAS

about 7 cups (1.75 L) **unbleached all-purpose flour**

1 ¹/₂ tbsp (22 mL) **kosher salt**

1 tbsp (15 mL) **active dry yeast**

3 cups (750 mL) **lukewarm water**, divided

In a small bowl, add the yeast to 1 cup (250 mL) lukewarm water. The water should be no warmer than a newborn baby's bath. Let it stand for 10 minutes, until the yeast has bubbled up. If the yeast has not bubbled up, it is dead and needs replacing.

Into a large stand mixer bowl, measure 6 cups (1.5 L) flour. Add the salt and stir well. Stir the yeast and add it to the mixing bowl along with 2 cups (500 mL) lukewarm water. Stir with a wooden spoon to combine. (If you are not using a stand mixer, mix the ingredients in a large bowl by hand using a wooden spoon.)

Fit the mixer with a dough hook and knead the dough at speed #2 for 5 minutes (or at the very lowest speed for 10 minutes). Add additional flour a spoonful at a time until the dough cleans the sides of the bowl. The dough should be slightly sticky. (Alternatively, knead the dough by hand on a lightly floured counter for 10 minutes.)

Remove dough hook. Remove dough and put 2 tsp (10 mL) vegetable oil into the bowl. Return the dough to the bowl and turn it over to fully coat it with the oil. Place the bowl into a plastic bag, and seal. Let the dough rise until doubled in bulk, about 1 ¹/₂ hours.

When the dough has risen, remove the bowl from the bag, and punch the dough down. Knead it several times on an unfloured counter. Invert the mixing bowl and place it over the dough for 10 minutes to allow the dough to relax.

Meanwhile, place a pizza stone in the bottom third of the oven. Preheat oven to 450°F (235°C).

Using a bench scraper or sharp knife, cut a chunk the size of a 2-inch (5 cm) ball from the dough. On a well-floured counter, roll out the dough to a circle about 7 inches (18 cm) in diameter. The dough should be fairly thin, about ¹/₈-inch (3 mm) thick. Roll out just enough pizza rounds to fit on your pizza stone. Let the prepared pizza bottoms rest uncovered for 10 minutes before topping and baking.

Use a peel to transfer the prepared pizzas to the preheated pizza stone in the oven and bake for 10 minutes, or until the top is bubbly and the edges are slightly brown. (If you don't have a peel, place the pizza bottoms on a well-floured, wooden cutting board before topping them, and then use a wide metal spatula to transfer the pizzas to the stone.)

Pizza Tip

I usually form another batch of pizza rounds and let them rest while the first batch is in the oven baking. Do not top them with sauce and toppings until just before they are to be baked or the dough will become too soft to transfer to the pizza stone and they will become soggy when baked.

Pizza Marinara

This fabulous, yet simple, uncooked tomato sauce comes from Gina Giambattista. Gina is a feisty little Italian woman, who, together with her son Carlo, owns the very popular Italian Star Deli in Regina. Gina never follows a recipe or measures anything, but she's very insistent on using the best ingredients. This is my version of her sauce, based on her "little bit of this" and "little bit of that" instructions. It tastes like a fragrant summer garden and it is my family's favourite. Many people have told me that pizzas made with this sauce taste just like the ones they ate in Italy. You can top it very simply, with a few slices of marinated artichoke hearts, a couple of buffalo mozzarella rounds, and a light sprinkling of grated cheese. This tomato sauce is also delicious tossed with fresh pasta for a quick meal.

MAKES ENOUGH TO TOP 18 7-INCH PIZZAS

Carlo and Gina
Giambattista.

1 batch **pizza dough** (recipe on facing page)

about 10 cups (2.5 L) shredded **cheese**, such as a mixture of mozzarella, provolone, medium cheddar and Parmesan

FRESH MARINARA SAUCE

1 can (28 oz/796 mL) **diced tomatoes**, preferably San Marsano

1 **fresh tomato**, very finely diced

1/4 cup (60 mL) **extra virgin olive oil**

1/4 cup (60 mL) chopped **fresh basil**

3 to 4 cloves **garlic**, peeled and minced

1 tsp (5 mL) **dried oregano**

1 tsp (5 mL) **dried basil**

1 tsp (5 mL) **kosher salt**

1/2 tsp (2 mL) freshly ground **black pepper**

1/4 tsp (1 mL) **chili flakes**

In a food processor bowl, pulse the canned tomatoes in an on-off motion until almost smooth. Scrape the mixture into a medium bowl and add the fresh tomato, olive oil, fresh basil, garlic, oregano, dried basil, salt, black pepper, and chili flakes. Stir well. Taste and adjust seasonings.

When the formed pizza rounds have rested, uncovered, for 10 minutes, spread each pizza round with about 3 tbsp (45 mL) of the uncooked tomato sauce. Top with any additional toppings and sprinkle with a small amount of grated cheese. Transfer the dressed pizzas to the hot pizza stone and bake for 10 minutes. Serve hot.

Leftover pizzas can be frozen.

Nouveaux Strawberries and Cream

This is the recipe that gave me my start in television. In the late 1990s, I wrote a food column for a small Ottawa newspaper. One day a local television producer noticed the recipe and invited me to come into the station and demonstrate it "live" for viewers. The next thing I knew, I was a morning regular, cooking my favourite recipes. Later, when I moved to Saskatchewan, it was the demo tape for this dessert that caught the eye of News Director Carl Worth when he was selecting a culinary host for CTV-Saskatchewan's run on *Good Morning Canada*. This dessert is easy and, despite the combination of ingredients not often associated with humble strawberries-and-cream, it tastes simply delicious. The key to its success is to buy excellent quality, aged balsamic vinegar at a specialty shop. Acidic supermarket varieties won't do.

SERVES 4 TO 6

1/2 cup (125 mL) **sliced almonds**

4 cups (1 L) washed, hulled, and quartered **fresh strawberries**

1 tbsp (15 mL) **brown sugar**

2 tbsp (30 mL) good quality aged **balsamic vinegar**

10 good grinds coarsely ground **black pepper**

1 oz (28 g) **semi-sweet** or bittersweet **chocolate**, grated or chopped

1 tub **premium vanilla ice cream**

Preheat oven to 350°F (180°C).

Toast the almonds on a cookie sheet for 5 to 7 minutes. Remove and set aside to cool.

In a large bowl, combine the prepared strawberries with the brown sugar, aged balsamic vinegar, and black pepper. Stir gently and let the berries macerate at room temperature for several hours. Stir occasionally to coat the strawberries with the syrup. Do not let the berries stand overnight or longer than a few hours because they will become soggy.

To serve, place one or two scoops of vanilla ice cream in a dessert dish. Top with a generous amount of the macerated strawberries. Sprinkle with the toasted almonds and grated chocolate.

Rhubarb Galette

This superb dessert shows off delicious spring rhubarb. The egg in the filling is the secret ingredient. It "softens" the tartness of the rhubarb. To make this recipe with sour cherries, increase the flour amount in the filling to $1/3$ cup (80 mL).

MAKES 1 LARGE FREE-FORM PIE

DOUGH

2 cups (500 mL) **unbleached all-purpose flour**

1 tsp (5 mL) **kosher salt**

1 tbsp (15 mL) **granulated sugar**

$1/2$ cup (125 mL) **cold butter**

3 tbsp (45 mL) **frozen all-vegetable shortening**

$1/3$ cup (80 mL), or more, **ice water**

FILLING

6 cups (1.5 L) **fresh rhubarb**, cleaned and cut into small pieces

$1/2$ cup (125 mL) **saskatoon berry jam**, blueberry jam, or strawberry jam

1 **egg**, beaten

$2/3$ cup (160 mL) **granulated sugar**

3 tbsp (45 mL) **unbleached all-purpose flour**

3 tsp (15 mL) **unsalted butter**

1 **egg**, beaten

1 tbsp (15 mL) **granulated sugar**

Preheat oven to 425°F (220°C).

DOUGH: In a large bowl, combine the flour, salt, and sugar; mix well. Using a box grater, grate in the cold butter and the frozen shortening. Sweep up some of the flour with the fat as you grate. Gather up some of the flour-fat mixture between your palms and rub in a downward motion once. Repeat 10 times, gathering up the flour-fat mixture each time (see photos on page 86).

Using a fork, mix in about $1/4$ cup (60 mL) ice water. Continue to add water in small amounts until the mixture feels slightly moist and begins to stick together.

On a floured surface, roll out the dough to a 16-inch (40 cm) circle using a floured rolling pin. Transfer the rolled dough to a parchment paper–lined pizza pan or cookie sheet.

FILLING AND ASSEMBLY: In a large bowl, mix together the fresh rhubarb, jam, beaten egg, granulated sugar, and 3 tbsp (45 mL) flour.

Pile the filling onto the centre of the prepared dough, leaving a 2-inch (5 cm) edge of exposed dough. Fold up sides over the filling, pleating as necessary to partially enclose filling; leave the top open. Dot with 3 tsp (15 mL) butter. Brush the dough edges with beaten egg and sprinkle with granulated sugar.

Bake the galette for 15 minutes, then reduce the heat to 350°F (180°C) and bake another 35 minutes. Let cool for 30 minutes, then slide the galette onto a flat serving platter. Serve warm or at room temperature.

Mixed Berry Shortcakes

Canadians adore shortcake. This version uses mixed berries—saskatoon berries, strawberries, raspberries, blackberries, or lingonberries. Adjust the mixture to suit whatever berries are in season. Replacing the usual whipped cream topping is a refreshing yogurt cream flavoured with vanilla and a hint of lemon. Allow plenty of time to make the Lemon-Yogurt Cream, as the yogurt requires at least 4 hours to drain and thicken.

SERVES 6 TO 8

LEMON-YOGURT CREAM

3 cups (750 mL) **plain 2% yogurt** with active bacterial culture and no thickeners or additives

3 tbsp (45 mL) **granulated sugar**

1 tbsp (15 mL) **vanilla extract**

finely grated **rind of half a lemon**

BERRY FILLING

5 cups (1.25 L) **mixed berries**, such as strawberries, raspberries, blackberries, saskatoon berries, or lingonberries

2 tbsp (30 mL) **granulated sugar**

SHORTCAKE BISCUITS

2 cups (500 mL) **unbleached all-purpose flour**

2 tbsp (30 mL) **granulated sugar**

1 tbsp (15 mL) **baking powder**

1 tsp (5 mL) **kosher salt**

finely grated **rind of half a lemon**

1/3 cup (80 mL) **cold unsalted butter**

1 cup (250 mL) **cold milk**

Unbleached All-Purpose Flour

I prefer to use unbleached all-purpose flour in my baking as bleached flour has undergone a "bleaching" process with a whitening agent to turn the flour white. Both flours provide the same quality results. Baked goods made with unbleached flour will have a slight ivory hue.

LEMON-YOGURT CREAM: Line a large sieve with several layers of cheesecloth. Set the sieve over, but not in, a large bowl. Spoon the yogurt into the lined sieve. Refrigerate and let drain at least 4 hours, preferably longer. Discard the whey liquid or use it to make bread.

After the yogurt has drained, transfer the thickened yogurt to a medium bowl and gently stir in the sugar, vanilla, and finely grated lemon rind. Refrigerate until ready to use.

BERRY FILLING: In a large bowl, combine the mixed berries with 2 tbsp (30 mL) granulated sugar. Let stand about 1 hour, stirring occasionally.

SHORTCAKE BISCUITS: Preheat oven to 400°F (200°C). Line a cookie sheet with parchment paper.

In a large bowl, combine the unbleached all-purpose flour, granulated sugar, baking powder, salt, and lemon rind. Using a box grater, grate in the butter, sweeping up some of the flour with the fat as you grate. Gather up some of the flour-fat mixture between your palms and rub in a downward motion once. Repeat 10 times, gathering up the flour-fat mixture each time (see photos on page 86).

Using a fork, stir in the cold milk until just combined. Transfer the dough to a lightly floured board and knead gently seven times, not more. Dough will come together into a ball.

Gently pat the dough into a circle about ³/₄-inch (2 cm) thick. Using a lightly floured round metal 2 ¹/₂ -inch (6.5 cm) cookie cutter, cut the dough into rounds, being careful not to twist the cookie cutter (twisting the cutter against the dough prevents the biscuit from rising high). Transfer the rounds to the parchment paper–lined cookie sheet. Continue to cut out all the dough. Scraps can be gently kneaded together once, and re-cut.

Bake for 15 minutes. Remove to a wire rack to cool.

ASSEMBLY: To serve, split each cooled shortcake biscuit in half. Set one half on a dessert plate. Top with some berries and a dollop of the Lemon-Yogurt Cream. Top with the other half of the biscuit and more berries.

Nearly ripe saskatoon berries at Very Berry Farm, White City, SK.

Old-Fashioned White Cake

If there's one cake that is made dozens of times throughout the year in our house, it's this one. My boys adore it. Over the years, I've made changes to the recipe: I now substitute the original part shortening-part butter amount with just butter, add almond extract, and use a mixture of yogurt and milk instead of plain milk for the liquid ingredients. This might just be the best white cake ever!

MAKES ONE 8-INCH (20 CM) SQUARE CAKE

1 1/2 cups (375 mL) **unbleached all-purpose flour**

2 1/2 tsp (12 mL) **baking powder**

1/2 tsp (2 mL) **kosher salt**

1/4 cup (60 mL) **plain yogurt***

1/2 cup (125 mL) **milk***

1/2 cup (125 mL) **unsalted butter**

1 cup (250 mL) **granulated sugar**

1/2 tsp (2 mL) **pure vanilla extract**

1/4 tsp (1 mL) **pure almond extract** (optional)

2 **eggs**

Preheat oven to 350°F (180°C). Grease and flour an 8-inch (20 cm) square cake pan.

Scoop the flour gently into the measuring cups. Level the top with the flat edge of a knife. Transfer the flour to a medium bowl and add the baking powder and salt. Stir to combine. Set aside.

Combine the yogurt and milk. Set aside.

In a mixer bowl, cream the butter with the sugar until creamy. Add the vanilla and almond extract. Add the eggs, one at a time, beating well after each addition. Add the dry ingredients alternately with the yogurt-milk mixture in three additions, ending with the dry ingredients. Turn the batter into the prepared pan.

Bake for 25 to 30 minutes, until a toothpick inserted into the centre comes out clean. Let cool completely and frost with a simple, vanilla buttercream icing, or serve the cake warm, topped with old-fashioned Brown Sugar Sauce (recipe follows).

* You can use 3/4 cup (185 mL) milk instead of the yogurt-milk combination.

Brown Sugar Sauce

1 cup (250 mL) packed **light brown sugar**

2 tbsp (30 mL) **cornstarch**

1/4 tsp (1 mL) **kosher salt**

2 cups (500 mL) **warm water**

2 tbsp (30 mL) **unsalted butter**

2 tsp (10 mL) **vanilla extract**

In a saucepan, combine the light brown sugar with the cornstarch and salt. Add warm water. Stir over low heat until thick and smooth. Remove from heat and add the butter and vanilla extract. Makes enough sauce for 8 servings.

Orange-Saffron Babycakes

Small desserts are all the rage. These cute little cakes can be dressed up all fancy for a dinner party or a little more understated for a romantic dinner for two. They are delicious either way.

MAKES 12

1 ½ cups (375 mL) **unbleached all-purpose flour**

2 ½ tsp (12 mL) **baking powder**

½ tsp (2 mL) **kosher salt**

¼ tsp (1 mL) **ground cinnamon**

pinch **saffron**

¾ cup (185 mL) **milk**

½ cup (125 mL) **unsalted butter**, room temperature

¾ cup (185 mL) **granulated sugar**

¼ cup (60 mL) **liquid honey**

½ tsp (2 mL) **vanilla extract**

finely grated **zest of 1 large orange**

2 **eggs**

Preheat oven to 350°F (180°C). Grease a 12-cup muffin pan.

Scoop the flour gently into the measuring cups. Level the top with the flat edge of a knife. Transfer the flour to a medium bowl and add the baking powder, salt, and cinnamon. Stir to combine. Set aside.

Finely grind the saffron in a small bowl. Add ¼ cup (60 mL) milk to the saffron and stir to combine well. Add the saffron-milk mixture to the remaining ½ cup (125 mL) milk. Set aside.

In a mixer bowl, cream the butter with the sugar and the honey until creamy. Add the vanilla and the orange zest. Add the eggs, one at a time, beating well after each egg is added. Add the dry ingredients alternately with the saffron-milk mixture in three additions, ending with the dry ingredients.

Turn the batter into the prepared muffin pan. Bake for 20 minutes, until a toothpick inserted into the centre comes out clean. Remove to a wire rack and let the cakes cool in the pan for 10 minutes. Remove the cakes and let cool completely. To serve, place cakes top side down onto a serving plate. Glaze with Icing Sugar Glaze.

Icing Sugar Glaze

2 cups (500 mL) **icing sugar**

¼ tsp (1 mL) **almond extract**

4 tbsp (60 mL) **milk**

Whisk icing sugar, almond extract, and milk until smooth, adding 1 tsp (5 mL) more milk if required. Drizzle over the inverted cakes and garnish as desired.

honey
LIQUID GOLD

We love honey. It's one of nature's sweet gifts. We spread it on our morning toast, stir it into tea, drizzle it on symbolic foods at festivals, and incorporate it into cold remedies. We add it to all manner of sweet and savoury cooking, and ferment it into a honey wine called mead.

Saskatchewan's 86,000 bee colonies are tended by 965 beekeepers. The town of Tisdale, located southeast of Prince Albert, is the Honey Capital of Saskatchewan. Apiaries there produce nearly half of Saskatchewan's honey production. Saskatchewan honeybees are among the hardest workers, zipping from flower to flower at up to 25 kilometres an hour, gathering pollen onto their back legs to produce more than 8,000 tonnes (17 million pounds) of the sticky stuff. That's a contribution to the Saskatchewan economy of $27 million every year, making the province the number two honey producer in Canada. Together, our little pollinators in the western provinces produce 80% of Canada's honey, with Alberta at 38%, Saskatchewan at 25%, and Manitoba at 17%.

TOP LEFT: Beekeeper Michelle Frischholz of Zee-Bee Honey in Zehner, SK, tends to her bees. Here she is holding a honey rack with eggs.

BOTTOM LEFT: Honeybees owned by Scott Lipsit, south of Prince Albert, SK.

RIGHT: A bee captures pollen from a clover blossom in the field behind my home.

Honey Spice Cookies

This is a superb little cookie from my childhood. It's crisp on the outside and chewy on the inside.

MAKES 3 DOZEN COOKIES

2 1/4 cups (560 mL) **unbleached all-purpose flour**

1 1/2 tsp (7 mL) **baking soda**

1/2 tsp (2 mL) **kosher salt**

1 tsp (5 mL) **ground ginger**

1/2 tsp (2 mL) **ground cinnamon**

1/4 tsp (1 mL) **ground cloves**

3/4 cup (185 mL) **all-vegetable shortening**

1 cup (250 mL) **brown sugar**

1 **egg**

1/4 cup (60 mL) **liquid honey** (not creamed)

water, for dipping

granulated sugar, for dipping

Preheat oven to 350°F (180°C). Line two cookie sheets with parchment paper.

Scoop the flour gently into the measuring cups. Level the top with the flat edge of a knife. Transfer the flour to a medium bowl and add the baking soda, salt, ginger, cinnamon, and cloves. Stir to combine. Set aside.

In a stand mixer, cream the shortening with the brown sugar until light. Add the egg and beat well. Add the honey. Mix to combine.

Add the dry ingredients all at once and mix well. Chill the dough for one hour, if desired.

Prepare a small bowl with about 1/4 cup (60 mL) cool water. Prepare a second small bowl with about 1/4 cup (60 mL) granulated sugar.

Roll the dough into small balls about 1 inch (2.5 cm) in diameter. Dip the top half in the water and then dip in the white sugar. Set the ball on the cookie sheet sugar side up, spacing each ball about 1 inch (2.5 cm) apart.

Bake for about 11 to 12 minutes, until the cookies are golden and slightly soft. Let cool for about 10 minutes and then remove to a cooling rack.

Triple-Chocolate Cookies

What can I say? My boys love 'em. My husband loves 'em. I love 'em. Yum!

MAKES ABOUT 5 DOZEN COOKIES

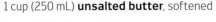

1 cup (250 mL) **unsalted butter**, softened

1 cup (250 mL) packed **brown sugar**

¼ cup (60 mL) **granulated sugar**

2 **eggs**

1½ tsp (7 mL) **pure vanilla extract**

1 cup (250 mL) **unbleached all-purpose flour**

1 cup (250 mL) **stone-ground whole wheat flour**

1 cup (250 mL) **quick-cooking rolled oats**

¼ cup (60 mL) sifted **cocoa**

1 tsp (5 mL) **baking soda**

½ tsp (2 mL) **kosher salt**

5 oz (140 g) **white chocolate**, such as Lindt, chopped into ⅜-inch (1 cm) squares

6 oz (170 g) **semi-sweet chocolate chips**

Preheat oven to 375°F (190°C). Line two cookie sheets with parchment paper.

Cream the butter, brown sugar, and granulated sugar until light. Add the eggs, one at a time, beating well after each addition. Add the vanilla and mix.

Scoop the all-purpose flour and the whole wheat flour gently into the measuring cups. Level the top with the flat edge of a knife. Transfer the flour to a medium bowl and add the rolled oats, cocoa, baking soda, and salt. Stir to combine.

Add the dry ingredients to the butter-sugar mixture and mix until just combined. With a wooden spoon, stir in the chopped white chocolate and semi-sweet chocolate pieces.

Drop by teaspoons onto cookie sheets, spacing the cookies several inches apart. Bake for about 12 minutes. Cool 10 minutes before removing the cookies to cooling rack.

Kosher Salt

Kosher salt is an additive-free, somewhat coarse, salt, with irregular-sized, flat crystals. Chefs prefer kosher salt because it has a clean taste and a less intense flavour. It's easy to "grab a pinch" to throw into a recipe. The recipes in this cookbook were developed using kosher salt. If you substitute table salt for kosher salt, use less salt than is called for in the recipe.

Muesli

Muesli is unsweetened, unbaked granola and is very popular in Europe. This recipe makes quite a bit. Freezing it will keep it fresh.

MAKES A HUGE BATCH

10 cups (2.5 L) **old-fashioned rolled oats**

1 cup (250 mL) **dried sour cherries**

1 cup (250 mL) **dried blueberries**

1 cup (250 mL) **dried cranberries**

1 cup (250 mL) **golden raisins**

2 cups (500 mL) **pumpkin seeds**

2 cups (500 mL) **dry-roasted sunflower seeds**

2 cups (500 mL) **sliced almonds**

2 cups (500 mL) **shredded sweetened coconut**

$^1/_2$ cup (125 mL) **sesame seeds**

Combine all the above ingredients in a large bowl. Mix together with your hands. Store in a large jar or in plastic zip-lock bags.

For a nutritious and filling breakfast, simply scoop $^1/_3$ to $^1/_2$ cup (80 to 125 mL) muesli into a bowl and enjoy with milk, almond milk, or plain yogurt and fruit.

Granola

This granola is a staple in our house. Have one bowl in the morning with plain yogurt and you'll feel full until lunch. This recipe makes a huge batch; freeze it for longer storage. Be sure to save some uncooked granola to make the Granola Bâtards on page 44.

MAKES A HUGE BATCH

1 cup (250 mL) **vegetable oil**

1 cup (250 mL) **maple syrup**

1 cup (250 mL) **liquid honey**

1 cup (250 mL) **unsweetened peanut butter**

14 cups (3.5 L) **large-flake old-fashioned rolled oats** (not quick or instant)

$1/4$ cup (60 mL) **hemp hearts** or sesame seeds

$1/3$ cup (80 mL) **flax seed**

3 $1/8$ cups (780 mL) hulled **sunflower seeds**

4 cups (1 L) roasted **whole soy nuts**

1 cup (250 mL) **sliced almonds**

1 cup (250 mL) toasted **pumpkin seeds**

2 tbsp (30 mL) **ground cinnamon**

1 tbsp (15 mL) **ground ginger**

2 cups (500 mL) **large shaved coconut**

3 cups (750 mL) assorted **dried fruit** (raisins, cranberries, sour cherries)

Preheat oven to 350°F (180°C).

In a microwave-safe bowl, combine the oil, maple syrup, liquid honey, and peanut butter. Microwave on high for 7 minutes. Stir with a whisk until well combined. (Alternatively, melt the mixture in a saucepan on the stove over medium-low heat.)

In a gigantic bowl, combine the oats, hemp hearts, flax seed, sunflower seeds, soy nuts, almonds, pumpkin seeds, cinnamon, and ginger. Stir to mix. Pour the oil–peanut butter mixture over the dry ingredients. Use a wooden spoon to combine well.

In batches, transfer the uncooked granola to a cookie sheet. Bake for 15 minutes. Stir and return to oven for 5 to 10 minutes. When golden brown, remove from oven and cool.

Add the coconut and dried fruit.

Granola Bâtards

A bâtard is a short, fat baguette. This recipe uses uncooked granola from the recipe on page 42. The combination of oatmeal, seeds, and nuts makes for a delicious bread.

MAKES TWO BÂTARDS

1 tbsp (15 mL) **traditional active dry yeast**

1 cup (250 mL) **lukewarm water**

2 cups (500 mL) **prepared uncooked granola** (recipe on page 42)

about 6 cups (1.5 L) **unbleached all-purpose flour**

1 ¹/₂ tbsp (22 mL) **kosher salt**

2 cups (500 mL) **lukewarm water**

1 tbsp (15 mL) **molasses**

In a small bowl, add the yeast to 1 cup (250 mL) lukewarm water. The water should be no warmer than a newborn baby's bath. Let it stand for 10 minutes, until the yeast has bubbled up. If the yeast has not bubbled up, it is dead and needs replacing.

In a large stand mixer bowl, combine the uncooked granola with 5 ¹/₂ cups (1375 mL) all-purpose flour, and salt. Stir with a wooden spoon to combine.

Stir the proofed yeast and add it to the flour mixture along with 2 cups (500 mL) lukewarm water and the molasses. Stir with a wooden spoon to combine.

Fit the mixer with a dough hook and knead the dough at speed #2 for 5 minutes (or on the very lowest speed for 10 minutes), adding additional flour a spoonful at a time until the dough cleans the sides of the bowl. The dough should be slightly sticky.

Remove the dough. Lightly grease the bowl with about 2 tsp (10 mL) oil and place dough back into the work bowl. Turn the dough to completely coat it with the oil. Place the bowl into a plastic bag and seal. Let the dough rise at room temperature for 1 ¹/₂ hours, or until doubled in size.

When the dough has risen, remove the bowl from the bag and punch the dough down. (At this point, you can refrigerate the dough until ready to form. Covered, it will last several days in the refrigerator. Bring the dough to room temperature before proceeding with the recipe.)

Knead the dough several times on an unfloured counter. Invert the mixing bowl and place it over the dough for 10 minutes to allow the dough to relax.

Using a bench scraper or sharp knife, cut the dough into two equal pieces. Roll each piece into a log 14 inches (35 cm) long and transfer the dough to a parchment paper–lined baking sheet. Cover and let rise for 30 to 40 minutes.

Meanwhile, preheat oven to 425°F (220°C). If you have one, place a pizza stone in the bottom third of the oven to preheat.

Dust the risen loaves lightly with flour and gently rub the flour over the loaves. Cut 4 or 5 diagonal slits in the top of each loaf, about ¹/₈ inch (3 mm) deep. Place the baking sheet with the loaves into the oven directly on the pizza stone, if using.

Place a pan with 2 cups (500 mL) of water on a rack in the oven to create a moist heat. This helps to make a nice crispy crust on the loaf.

Bake at 425°F (220°C) for 15 minutes, then lower heat to 350°F (180°C) and bake for another 20 minutes. Remove the loaves from the baking sheet and place them on a wire rack to cool.

Hot days. Satin-blue skies,

Patchwork fields of yellow, and violet, and green,

Farmers' markets laden with local bounty,

Kitchens sticky with warm sweet pickles 'n' berry jams.

Lazy backyard barbeques smell of smoky burgers, steaks.

Wild-forest buffets of mushrooms, berries, nuts,

Stocked lakes shimmer in the midday sun...

The time to reap.

The time to eat.

A field of canola in full bloom outside Drinkwater, SK.

summer

Roasted Tomato and Vegetable Soup

This recipe concentrates the flavours of summer, with roasted vegetables cooked in a delicious stock, then puréed into a velvety soup. Like a good stew, this soup is best when made a day ahead.

SERVES 6

2 to 3 lbs (907 g to 1.36 kg) **fresh vine-ripened tomatoes**, stems removed and halved

6 cloves **garlic**, peeled and left whole

2 **onions**, peeled and sliced into thick slices

1/2 lb (227 g) peeled **carrots**, cut into 1-inch (2.5 cm) chunks

1 **red pepper**, halved

vegetable oil, for drizzling

1 to 2 tsp (5 to 10 mL) **dried thyme** or Italian seasoning

4 to 5 cups (1 L to 1.25 L) **chicken stock**

10 oz (284 mL) **evaporated milk**

salt and **pepper**, to taste

Garden-fresh tomatoes at a farmers' market.

Preheat oven to 400°F (200°C).

Oil two rimmed cookie sheets. Lay tomatoes cut side up. Add the whole garlic cloves, onion slices, and carrots. Lay the red pepper cut side down. Drizzle with oil, and sprinkle with salt, pepper, and dried thyme.

Roast the vegetables for 30 to 40 minutes, or until they are lightly browned and the skin starts to shrink back from the tomatoes.

Remove the cookie sheets from the oven and let the vegetables cool slightly. Peel the skin off the tomatoes and the pepper halves and discard. Roughly chop the peppers.

In a large Dutch oven or stockpot, bring the chicken stock to a boil. Add all the roasted vegetables. Bring to a boil; reduce heat and let simmer 20 minutes.

Purée the mixture in batches in a blender or food processor, then return the soup to the pot. (Or use a hand immersion blender and purée the soup directly in the pot.)

Add the evaporated milk. Heat through but do not boil. Taste and adjust seasonings.

Spicy Vegetable Bean Soup

This is a hearty, main dish soup with just a nice amount of spice. It's delicious topped with a spoonful of yogurt to take the edge off the heat.

SERVES 8 TO 10

2 tbsp (30 mL) **vegetable oil**

1 large **onion**, peeled and diced

2 cloves **garlic**, peeled and finely chopped

1 **leek**, sliced lengthwise, and then sliced into ¼-inch (5 mm) wide slices

2 **carrots**, peeled and diced into ¼-inch (5 mm) cubes

½ tsp (2 mL) **kosher salt**

½ tsp (2 mL) **black pepper**

1 **red pepper**, diced into ¼-inch (5 mm) cubes

2 tsp (10 mL) **ground cumin**

1 tsp (5 mL) **ground turmeric**

1 tsp (5 mL) **ground coriander**

1 tsp (5 mL) **dried thyme leaves**

½ tsp (2 mL) **ground cinnamon**

2 very finely diced **Thai red chili peppers** with seeds; or 1 tsp (5 mL) dried chili flakes

1 can (28 oz/796 mL) **diced tomatoes**

6 cups (1.5 L) **chicken** or vegetable **stock**

1 can (19 oz/540 mL) **black beans**, drained and rinsed

thick plain yogurt, for garnish

In a large Dutch oven or stockpot over low heat, add the oil, then the onion, garlic, and leek. Cover and sweat the mixture over low heat for about 5 minutes, stirring occasionally.

Add the carrots, salt, and pepper. Cover and continue to sweat the vegetables for another 5 minutes, stirring occasionally.

Add the red pepper, cover and sweat 10 minutes, stirring occasionally.

In a small bowl, combine the cumin, turmeric, ground coriander, thyme, cinnamon, and chili peppers. Add these to the cooked vegetable mixture and sauté, stirring constantly, for one minute to toast the spices.

Add the diced tomatoes, chicken stock, and black beans. Bring to a boil, reduce heat, and let simmer, uncovered, for 20 minutes. Taste and add additional salt and pepper, if necessary.

Ladle the soup into bowls and top with a dollop of thick plain yogurt.

Curried Vegetable Soup with Orzo

You might wonder about the Italian orzo pasta in this Indian-style soup, but it works perfectly. Orzo pasta is shaped like grains of white rice. You can substitute white rice, but the consistency of the soup won't be quite the same. This is a great soup to serve when you're trying to introduce a soup lover to something new and slightly exotic. Try the Thai variation, too (see sidebar).

SERVES 6 TO 8

2 **onions**, diced

2 **carrots**, diced into ¹/₂-inch (1.5 cm) cubes

1 stalk **celery**, diced into
¹/₂-inch (1.5 cm) cubes

2 tbsp (30 mL) **vegetable oil**

1 tbsp (15 mL) **Indian-style curry paste**, or curry powder

4 cups (1 L) **chicken stock**

1 can (28 oz/796 mL) **diced tomatoes**

¹/₂ cup (125 mL) **orzo pasta**

14 oz (400 mL) **coconut milk**

2 tbsp (30 mL) chopped **fresh cilantro**

Thai Variation

Substitute Thai yellow curry paste for the Indian-style curry paste. Together with the coconut milk, add 1 tbsp (15 mL) brown sugar, and 1 tbsp (15 mL) fish sauce. Taste and adjust seasonings.

In a large Dutch oven or stockpot, sauté the onions, carrots, and celery in the oil over medium heat until soft, about 7 minutes. Add the curry paste and cook, stirring constantly, for 1 to 2 minutes. Add the chicken stock, tomatoes, and orzo pasta. Bring to a boil. Reduce heat and let simmer, uncovered, for 20 minutes. Add the coconut milk and fresh cilantro. Heat through, but do not boil. Serve with crusty bread.

Mushroom Cappuccino Soup

This fabulous soup captures the flavour of our favourite forest find. The trick to this soup is to be patient and cook the mushrooms until all their water has been cooked off. If you have access to local wild mushrooms, try using a selection of chanterelle, morel, and matsutake mushrooms for all or some of the mushrooms in this recipe. Enjoy this soup as a creative starter to a dinner party. Frothing the milk and garnishing each cup with mushroom dust gives the soup the look of a cappuccino.

SERVES 4

Mushroom Dust

To make mushroom dust, place about 1 oz (28 g) dried mushrooms in a blender. Process to a powder.

2 tbsp (30 mL) **unsalted butter**

3 $^1/_2$ oz (100 g) **fresh shiitake mushrooms**, stems removed, sliced

3 $^1/_2$ oz (100 g) **fresh oyster mushrooms**, sliced

7 oz (200 g) **fresh cremini (brown) mushrooms**, or button mushrooms, sliced

2 **shallots**, peeled and diced, about 2 tbsp (30 mL)

$^1/_2$ cup (125 mL) diced **onion**

1 clove **garlic**, minced

$^1/_2$ tsp (2 mL) **kosher salt**

2 cups (500 mL) full-flavoured **chicken stock**

$^1/_4$ tsp (1 mL) **dried thyme leaves**

$^1/_2$ cup (125 mL) **cream** (35% or half and half), optional

$^1/_4$ cup (60 mL) **chicken stock** or water, if required

$^1/_2$ cup (125 mL) **milk**, for frothing

1 tbsp (15 mL) **mushroom dust** for garnish (see sidebar)

In a saucepan over medium-low heat, melt the butter. Add the shiitake, oyster, and cremini mushrooms, along with the shallots, onion, garlic, and salt. Stir to combine, and cover. Let the mixture sweat for 10 minutes, stirring occasionally. Remove the lid and let the mixture slowly cook until all the liquid has been absorbed, about 10 minutes.

Add the chicken stock and the thyme. Stir and bring to a boil. Reduce the heat and simmer, uncovered, for 5 minutes.

Transfer the mixture to a blender or food processor and process until smooth. Return the soup to the pot and add the cream and additional stock or water, if necessary. The soup should have body and not be thin. Taste and adjust the seasonings. Reheat but do not boil.

Meanwhile, in a small saucepan over medium heat, heat the milk to almost the boiling point, whisking constantly and vigorously. This will aerate the milk and create a layer of foam on top of the warmed milk.

Ladle the soup into cappuccino cups, filling about $^7/_8$ full. To each cup, add about 1 tbsp (15 mL) of the warm milk and then gently add a spoonful or two of foam, dividing it equally. Garnish with a pinch of mushroom dust.

Sautéed Chanterelles

Wild mushrooms grow in every province in Canada. Among the most sought-after in the world are chanterelles that grow in Saskatchewan. You know them by their beautiful yellowy-orange colour, trumpet shape, and the gill-like ridges that run almost to the base of the stem. They have a very distinct flavour of earthy forest, apricots, and mild pepper. Chefs adore them. The best way to serve chanterelles is to cook them very simply with butter, salt, pepper, and perhaps a splash of fresh cream.

SERVES 4

8 oz (225 g) whole **fresh chanterelles**, about 3 cups (750 mL)

2 tbsp (30 mL) **unsalted butter**

¹/₂ tsp (2 mL) **kosher salt**, or to taste

few grinds of **black pepper**

Clean the mushrooms with a pastry brush. Over medium heat, melt the butter in a medium skillet. When the butter is melted and beginning to foam, add the cleaned chanterelles. Cover with a lid, reduce the heat slightly, and let the mushrooms cook for several minutes during which time they will release quite a bit of water. After about 5 minutes, remove the lid, and let the mushrooms simmer until all the liquid has evaporated. Sprinkle with salt and pepper.

Serve hot with just about any protein, such as wild game, chicken, steak, or grilled fish.

Puff Pastry Cups

Preheat oven to 400°F (200°C). On a floured board, roll out defrosted puff pastry to about ¹/₈ inch (3 mm) thickness. Using a pastry cutter cut out 3-inch (7.5 cm) rounds and place them on a parchment paper–lined cookie sheet. Using a sharp paring knife or small cookie cutter, score a small circle about ¹/₂ inch (1.5 cm) from the edge of each round, being careful not to cut all the way through the dough. Prick the inside circle all over with a fork. Bake about 8 to 10 minutes until golden. Transfer cups to a wire rack to cool. With a paring knife, cut out and remove the centres to form cavities and fill as desired. A standard 14-oz (400 g) package of puff pastry should make 12 pastry cups.

Creamed Chanterelles in a Pastry Cup

Dress up these delicious mushrooms by serving them creamed in a pastry cup. Garnish with a sprig of fresh parsley.

SERVES 6

6 **pre-baked pastry cups**, purchased or homemade (see sidebar)

1 recipe **Sautéed Chanterelles** (recipe above)

¹/₄ cup (60 mL) **35% cream**

salt and **pepper**, to taste

6 sprigs of **fresh parsley**, for garnish

Prepare the Sautéed Chanterelles (recipe above). When the liquid has evaporated, add the cream, salt, and pepper, to taste. Simmer for several minutes until the cream has thickened.

Spoon the hot mushroom mixture into baked pastry cups and garnish each portion with a sprig of fresh parsley. Serve hot.

Morel

Chanterelles

56

Honey Mushrooms

Honey Mushroom

mushrooms
NATURE'S TREASURE

The wild mushroom could easily be considered the caviar of Saskatchewan. It is highly sought-after, rare, and expensive, a culinary delicacy that is above comparison with the humble supermarket button mushroom.

Hand-picked, sometimes hundreds of miles from the nearest airstrip, wild mushrooms land on the cutting boards of the finest Canadian, European, and Japanese chefs within forty-eight hours of harvesting. And like those chefs, who pay big bucks for these forest jewels, restaurant-goers shell out handsomely for gourmet pizza topped with sun-dried tomatoes and sliced pine mushrooms; creamy risotto infused with white wine, garlic, and pungent morels; and rich braised beef stew studded with golden chanterelles.

The Saskatchewan wild mushroom industry is worth about $1 million annually; it employs between four hundred and five hundred pickers. Just for a few short months each summer and fall, these pickers will comb the boreal forest around La Ronge and fill basket after basket with these forest gems.

Among the most sought-after is the chanterelle, and northern Saskatchewan chanterelles are reputed to be among those of the highest quality in the world. It is my favourite mushroom. These beautiful, apricot-coloured trumpets are firm, aromatic, and clean of any debris. They begin to appear in late July and early August and often can be found right up to the first hard frost. They have a unique flavour and are best enjoyed when prepared very simply: with salt and pepper, a little butter, and perhaps a splash of cream.

Also highly desirable, morels are the first mushroom to appear in spring. They begin to poke through in the first weeks of May, when just a few patches of melting snow remain and crocuses are beginning to emerge. Among the first is the black morel, followed by the common morel. These varieties can be found just about anywhere, even in newly constructed urban areas. Indeed, morels grow all over North America and they all share an exceptional taste.

The province is also rich in other wild mushrooms. A few of the most common are the matsutake, or pine mushroom; "king" boletus, or cep mushroom; and the pidpenky, or honey mushroom. The pidpenky is highly prized by Ukrainians and is traditionally served at Christmas in a creamy sauce. Even the common store-bought button mushroom, as well as the cremini and portobello, grow in Saskatchewan.

Sadly, many of us have lost our connection to wild mushrooms, one of the true local foods. Unless you're a picker or know a picker, it is difficult to obtain these forest fungi, since they can't be purchased in stores or at farmers' markets in Saskatchewan. Virtually every last trumpet-shaped chanterelle, spongy morel, and toadstool-looking pine mushroom is shipped to high-end restaurants and consumer markets across the country, or into Europe or Japan. To add to the sting, many of the pretty packages of exotic dried mushrooms that cost a small fortune in local grocery stores are indeed Saskatchewan mushrooms.

However, if you should have the opportunity to enlist the services of a mushroom expert who can guide you in distinguishing edible mushrooms from those that are toxic, I wholeheartedly recommend taking an afternoon, switching off your cell phone, and following your mushroom guide: you'll be amazed to find these exquisite delicacies just about anywhere. With any luck, you'll return home with a newfound connection to nature and its bounty, and with some delicious additions to your table.

57

Mushroom-Chèvre Phyllo Triangles

Here is a fun appetizer that showcases wonderful forest mushrooms and earthy goat cheese. Serve them as they are, or try them atop a simple, tossed mixed-greens salad with a malt-basil vinaigrette.

MAKES 8 LARGE TRIANGLES

2 oz (56 g) creamy mild **chèvre** (goat cheese)

7 oz (200 g) **mushrooms**, such as cremini, button, shiitake, or chanterelles

2 tbsp (30 mL) **unsalted butter**

1 clove **garlic**, minced

1 tbsp (15 mL) finely chopped **shallots**

pinch **kosher salt**

pinch **dried sage**

1 tbsp (15 mL) **apple brandy** or cognac

1/8 tsp (.5 mL) freshly ground **black pepper**

4 sheets **phyllo dough**, defrosted in the refrigerator overnight

1/4 cup (60 mL) **olive oil**

4 tbsp (60 mL) **ground almonds**

Line a cookie sheet with parchment paper. Set aside.

Place the chèvre in the freezer to firm up, about 15 minutes.

Meanwhile, clean the mushrooms. Quarter them and slice them crosswise thinly.

Heat the butter in a medium skillet over medium heat. Add the garlic, shallots, salt, sage, and prepared mushrooms. Sauté until all the moisture has cooked off. Add the brandy or cognac and the black pepper. Sauté another minute or so, and remove the skillet from the heat. Cool the mixture to room temperature. When the mixture has cooled, crumble the chèvre into the mixture and gently fold together. You should still have small clumps of cheese visible in the mixture.

Preheat oven to 400°F (200°C).

Unwrap the phyllo and lay it on a clean counter. Cover it with a lightly damp tea towel to prevent it from drying out. Set out the olive oil, a pastry brush, and the ground almonds.

Remove one sheet of phyllo dough at a time, keeping the remainder covered with the damp tea towel. Brush the sheet lightly with olive oil, then sprinkle with about 1 1/2 tbsp (22 mL) ground almonds. Cover with another sheet of phyllo. Using a pizza cutter or sharp knife, cut the pastry in half crosswise. Cut each half in half crosswise again to create four strips.

Place a heaping tablespoon of filling about 1/2 inch (1.5 cm) from the bottom of each strip. Fold the bottom pastry up to partially cover the filling. Fold the pastry over to the right to encase the filling and create a triangular pastry. Continue to fold up the triangle as if you were folding a flag, first to the left, then up, then to the right, to form a triangle. Brush the outside with oil and sprinkle with a small amount of ground almonds. Set the triangle on the parchment-lined cookie sheet. Repeat with the remaining three strips.

Continue layering two more sheets of phyllo, and folding the phyllo and filling to create four more triangles. Bake for 10 minutes. Serve warm.

Crunchy Broccoli Salad

This tasty salad with a dash of Asian flair is a terrific side dish at any time of the year.

SERVES 4 TO 6

4 tsp (20 mL) **liquid honey**

4 tsp (20 mL) **Asian sesame oil**

²/₃ cup (160 mL) **vegetable oil**

4 tbsp (60 mL) **rice wine vinegar**

2 tbsp (30 mL) **soy sauce**

2 cloves **garlic**, peeled and minced

1 head **broccoli**, cut into small florets and ¹/₂-inch (1.5 cm) pieces

2 **carrots**, peeled, halved lengthwise, and cut on the diagonal

half a **red onion**, halved and sliced

2 stalks **celery**, sliced on the diagonal

1 cup (250 mL) **almonds**, slivered or sliced, and toasted

In a large salad bowl, whisk together the honey, sesame oil, vegetable oil, rice wine vinegar, soy sauce, and garlic. Add the broccoli, carrots, red onion, celery, and almonds. Toss well. Marinate about 1 hour before serving.

Spicy Tomato and Cucumber Salad

The key to this tasty salad is to layer in the flavours by seasoning the salad as it is being prepared, rather than at the end.

SERVES 4

3 to 4 large **tomatoes**, diced

half to 1 whole **English cucumber**, seeded and diced

half a **white** or red **onion**, halved and thinly sliced

1 **green finger hot pepper**, Thai red chili pepper, or jalapeño pepper, minced (seeds included)

about 1 tsp (5 mL) **kosher salt**, divided

2 to 3 tsp (10 to 15 mL) **ground cumin**

black pepper, to taste

juice of 1 fresh lime, or to taste

handful chopped **fresh cilantro**

Assemble this salad just before serving.

In a bowl, combine tomatoes, cucumber, and onion. Sprinkle with salt, and toss gently. Add the hot pepper. Toss again. Add the cumin, black pepper, and lime juice, and toss again. Taste, and add more salt or other seasonings, if required. Garnish with fresh cilantro and serve immediately. This salad does not store well.

61

Fried Green Tomatoes

After having watched the movie of the same name years ago, I just had to try my hand at this southern-U.S. dish. Every summer, we now look forward to a stash of green tomatoes to fry up and enjoy with a variety of meals. Green tomatoes are tart and firm and need a longer cooking time than do sweet, ripe tomatoes.

SERVES 4

4 **green tomatoes**, stems removed and sliced into ³/₈-inch (1 cm) wide slices

¹/₄ cup (60 mL) **unbleached all-purpose flour**

¹/₄ cup (60 mL) **cornmeal**

1 tsp (5 mL) **kosher salt**

1 tsp (5 mL) **granulated sugar**

1 tsp (5 mL) **dried thyme**

freshly ground **black pepper**, to taste

1 **egg**, beaten

¹/₂ cup (125 mL) **milk**

vegetable oil, for frying

Preheat a cast-iron or heavy metal skillet over medium heat.

In a plastic bag, combine the flour, cornmeal, salt, sugar, dried thyme, and pepper.

In a separate bowl, whisk together the egg and milk.

Add just enough oil to cover the bottom of the skillet.

Dip the sliced tomatoes into the egg-milk mixture and then into the flour-cornmeal mixture. Fry for several minutes per side until tender but not too soft; transfer to a paper towel to drain.

Serve while warm and crispy.

Slow-Roasted Tomatoes

Canning isn't the only way to preserve the taste of summer. Like no other preserving method, roasting slowly in the oven intensifies the taste of tomatoes. And for those of you who don't have the time or the inclination to spend an afternoon skinning tomatoes and sterilizing jars, this is an easy option that works while you sleep at night. These tomatoes are delicious when tossed in pasta, added to dips, sliced into salads, or enjoyed as part of an antipasto tray (try the Prairie Antipasto Platter on page 102).

MAKES 36 TOMATO HALVES

18 **Roma tomatoes**

dried basil

dried oregano

smoked paprika (optional)

freshly ground **black pepper**

kosher salt

extra virgin olive oil

Preheat oven to 200°F (93°C).

Line two baking sheets with parchment paper.

Wash and dry the tomatoes. Cut each tomato in half lengthwise. Remove the core at the top of the tomato. Deseed the tomatoes, if you like, although this is not necessary (see sidebar). Place tomatoes, cut side up, in a single layer on the baking sheets.

Sprinkle with dried basil, dried oregano, smoked paprika, pepper, and salt. Drizzle with olive oil. Place in the oven for 6 to 8 hours. You can put the tomatoes in just when you go to bed and remove them from the oven when you wake up. The longer they stay in the oven the drier they become. The tomatoes will have shrunk somewhat when they are finished. (If you find that your oven gets too warm, even at the lowest setting, leave the oven door slightly open to allow the heat to escape.) Remove the tomatoes from the oven and cool completely.

To store, place the roasted tomatoes in a sterilized jar* and cover with 1 inch (2.5 cm) olive oil. Store in the refrigerator for 1 to 3 months. Alternatively, place the dried tomatoes on a baking sheet in a single layer and freeze. Remove when frozen and place the frozen tomatoes in zip-lock bags and return to the freezer. Remove tomatoes as needed. They will take about 15 minutes to thaw.

To sterilize a jar: Place a clean jar and its lid in a large pot of boiling water and boil for 10 minutes.

Roasted Tomatoes Tip

If you remove the seeds, your roasted tomatoes will be plump and juicier. Deseeded tomatoes taste best when the skins are removed. Just pinch the skin with your fingers when the tomatoes have cooked and cooled slightly. It will slip off quite easily.

If you don't remove the seeds, your roasted tomatoes will be more shrunken and fairly small. You do not need to remove the skins.

Spicy Chipotle Bison Burgers

This burger is updated with smoky modern flavours.

SERVES 4

1 **red pepper**

1 to 1 ¹/₂ lb (454 to 680 g) **ground bison**

salt and **pepper**, to taste

1 **white onion**, sliced into thick slices

4 **hamburger buns**, toasted

4 **leaf lettuce** leaves

4 slices **havarti** or provolone **cheese** (optional)

Preheat barbeque.

Roast the red pepper by setting the whole red pepper directly on the barbeque grate over medium-high heat. Close lid. Turn the pepper occasionally until it is completely charred and black. Remove to a plate. Cut a slit in the pepper to release the hot steam and let stand until cool enough to handle. Peel off and discard the thin black skin; discard the stem and seeds. Cut the pepper into quarters. Set aside.

Form the meat into four patties; salt and pepper both sides. Place the bison patties and thick onion slices on the grill and grill over medium heat until the onion slices are golden brown and the bison patties are just barely cooked through. The key to a juicy burger is to turn the patties only once and never press on them with the back of the spatula.

To serve, spread a generous amount of Spicy Chipotle Mayo on the inside of a toasted hamburger bun. Top with a bison patty, then one grilled onion slice, one quarter of the roasted red pepper, a cheese slice, and lettuce. Top with the burger bun.

Spicy Chipotle Mayo

1 cup (250 mL) **mayonnaise**

1 to 2 **chipotle peppers** with adobo sauce, finely chopped, or 1 to 2 tbsp (15 to 30 mL) chipotle-flavoured hot sauce, or to taste

1 clove **garlic**, minced

1 tsp (5 mL) **ground cumin**

1 tbsp (15 mL) chopped **cilantro**

In a medium bowl, whisk together the mayonnaise, chipotle pepper, garlic, cumin, and cilantro. Refrigerate until ready to use.

Blue Cheese Lamb Burgers with Garlic Mayo

Prairie lamb is so mild, even the pickiest lamb eater will enjoy these burgers. The flavours of the blue cheese and rosemary along with the Garlic Mayo are a perfect match.

MAKES 4 BURGERS

1 lb (454 g) **ground lamb**

1/2 tsp (2 mL) **black pepper**

1/2 tsp (2 mL) **kosher salt**

1 tbsp (15 mL) chopped **fresh rosemary**, or 1 tsp (5 mL) crushed dried rosemary

2 **green onions**, trimmed and finely sliced

1/2 cup (125 mL) crumbled **blue cheese**, or to taste

1 tbsp (15 mL) **Dijon mustard**

4 **hamburger buns**

4 slices **white onion**

4 **leaf lettuce** leaves or fresh deli sprouts, such as radish or broccoli

Preheat barbeque.

    In a medium bowl, combine the ground lamb with the pepper, salt, fresh rosemary, green onions, blue cheese, and Dijon mustard. Using your hands, mix well. Form into four hamburger patties. (Patties can be prepared to this point and refrigerated until ready to use. Remove them from the refrigerator 30 minutes prior to cooking.)

    Oil the barbeque grates and place patties on the hot grill. Grill the patties, turning once, to desired doneness.

    Serve on toasted hamburgers buns topped with white onion slices, lettuce leaves or sprouts, and the Garlic Mayo.

Garlic Mayo

3 cloves **garlic**, minced

1/4 tsp (1 mL) **kosher salt**

1 cup (250 mL) **mayonnaise**

1 1/2 tsp (7 mL) **fresh lemon juice**

1 tsp (5 mL) **Dijon mustard**

1 tsp (5 mL) chopped **fresh parsley**

1 tbsp (15 mL) **olive oil**

With a mortar and pestle, mash together the minced garlic and salt. Transfer to a small bowl and whisk in the mayonnaise, fresh lemon juice, Dijon mustard, fresh parsley, and olive oil. Let stand about 30 minutes to allow the flavours to develop. Chill until ready to use.

Orange-Spiced Lamb Kebabs

Lamb is a perfect canvas for exotic spices. Bring the flavours of the Middle East to your prairie table with this simple but delicious kebab recipe.

SERVES 4

1 lb (454 g) tender **lamb meat**, such as from the leg, trimmed

¼ cup (60 mL) chopped **fresh cilantro**

2 cloves **garlic**, minced

2 tbsp (30 mL) **olive oil**

½ tsp (2 mL) **ground cinnamon**

½ tsp (2 mL) **ground black pepper**

¼ tsp (1 mL) **ground allspice**

¼ tsp (1 mL) **ground cardamom**

finely grated **zest of 1 orange**

juice of half an orange

Cut lamb into 1-inch (2.5 cm) cubes.

To make the marinade, in a small bowl, stir together the cilantro, garlic, olive oil, ground cinnamon, black pepper, allspice, cardamom, orange zest, and orange juice.

Place the cubed lamb into a large zip-lock bag and pour the marinade over it. Seal and toss to coat the meat. Refrigerate several hours or overnight.

Thread the lamb cubes onto skewers. (If the skewers are wooden, presoak them in water for 1 hour.)

GRILL PAN METHOD: Heat the pan over medium-high heat. Add a little vegetable oil and place the kebabs in the hot pan. Grill, turning occasionally, until medium rare or to desired doneness.

BARBEQUE METHOD: Heat the barbeque to medium-high. Lightly oil grates and place the kebabs on the grates over direct heat. Grill about 7 to 10 minutes, until medium rare, or to desired doneness.

Let the cooked kebabs rest, loosely covered, for about 10 minutes prior to serving.

Serve with rice or couscous, and a tossed salad.

prairie lamb
UNPARALLELED TASTE AND TENDERNESS

We may be the fourth-largest sheep-producing province, but from a chef's perspective, Saskatchewan lamb is number one. It's tender and has a delicate flavour unlike any other. I love it!

Sheep were first introduced to the province in the early 1800s, and Saskatchewan's sheep and lambs still graze in the wide-open expanse of the southern prairie grasslands. Wild herbs, prairie grasses, and grain, as well as the ever-blowing prairie winds and glorious sunshine, contribute to the meat's fabulous flavour. Try this delicious prairie meat gently braised in a chickpea curry, grilled with Moroccan spices, or roasted with lots of garlic and rosemary. Most cuts of lamb should be cooked to medium, or medium rare, to take advantage of the flavour and tenderness, as well as the food value: lamb is an excellent source of protein, iron, zinc, and B vitamins. Although the majority of Saskatchewan lamb is shipped out of province for slaughter, Canadian lamb, no matter where it's raised, has a similar flavour. If you truly want to buy lamb grown on the prairies, establish a relationship with a local farmer. By buying locally you will experience a vital connection to your food.

TOP: Sheep often graze in a mixed flock, such as here alongside Dexter cattle and llamas at Lumsden Sheep, Lumsden, SK.

BOTTOM LEFT: Lumsden Sheep, Lumsden, SK.

BOTTOM RIGHT: My son Ben bottle feeds a lamb at Farmgate Food, near Balgonie, SK.

68

Indian-Inspired Lamb Chops

Rubs are a great way to add flavour without adding calories. This pungent rub is also delicious on chicken.

SERVES 4

SPICE RUB

1 tbsp (15 mL) **brown sugar**	1 tsp (5 mL) **black pepper**
2 tsp (10 mL) **garam masala**	1/2 tsp (2 mL) **chili powder**
1 tsp (5 mL) **ground cumin**	1/2 tsp (2 mL) **onion powder**
1 tsp (5 mL) **kosher salt**	1/2 tsp (2 mL) **cayenne powder**

8 to 10 **lamb chops**, cut 1-inch (2.5 cm) thick	1 tbsp (15 mL) finely chopped **parsley**, for garnish
olive oil, for drizzling	

Preheat barbeque.

To make the spice rub, combine the brown sugar, garam masala, ground cumin, salt, black pepper, chili powder, onion powder, and cayenne powder in a small bowl. Mix well.

Drizzle the lamb chops on both sides with oil. Coat both sides of the chops liberally with the spice rub and massage it into the meat.

Grill over medium-high heat until medium rare, or to desired doneness. Remove and let rest, loosely covered, for 10 minutes.

Transfer the chops to a serving platter and sprinkle with parsley. Serve with your favourite red pepper jelly or mango chutney.

Goat Cheese and Red Pepper-Stuffed Chicken Breasts

Goat cheese, also called chèvre, is being produced across the Prairies, including most recently in Saskatchewan. Chèvre is a wonderfully earthy and clean-tasting cheese. For this recipe, be sure to purchase the creamy and spreadable variety. Purchase a jar of roasted red peppers, or prepare them yourself using the recipe on page 103.

SERVES 4 TO 6

4 boneless, skinless **chicken breasts**

3 **roasted red peppers**, peeled and deseeded

$^1/_2$ cup (125 mL) **goat cheese** (chèvre), plain or flavoured

several bunches of **fresh basil**, stems removed

salt and **pepper**, to taste

vegetable oil, for frying

$^1/_2$ cup (125 mL) **dry red wine**

1 cup (250 mL) **chicken stock**

1 tbsp (15 mL) **cold butter**

butcher twine to tie the chicken breasts

Preheat oven to 400°F (200°C).

Place chicken breast between two pieces of waxed paper. Using a meat mallet or rolling pin, pound the breast to about $^1/_4$-inch (5 mm) thickness.

Cut the roasted red peppers into quarters.

Lay the chicken breasts on a clean counter. Spread 1 to 2 tbsp (15 to 30 mL) goat cheese on the upside of each breast to completely cover. Top with a single layer of basil leaves, spreading out each leaf so it lies flat. Top the basil with the red peppers. Sprinkle with salt and pepper.

Roll up each breast into a pinwheel-style log. Using butcher twine, tie each breast closed. Sprinkle with salt and pepper.

Preheat a large skillet with an ovenproof handle* on high heat. Add about 1 tbsp (15 mL) oil, and sear each breast on all sides, until golden brown but not fully cooked through.

Transfer the skillet to the hot oven. Roast the chicken breasts for about 12 minutes. Transfer the breasts to a platter. Cover with a single layer of waxed paper and then cover with a tea towel. Let the breasts rest about 10 minutes before slicing.

Meanwhile, place the same skillet with the pan drippings over medium heat. Deglaze the pan with the red wine. Let the wine simmer until reduced by half. Add the chicken stock and simmer until reduced by half. Whisk in the cold butter. Season with salt and pepper.

To serve, remove the butcher twine from each breast. Cut the breasts into $^1/_2$-inch (1.5 cm) thick slices. Spoon a small pool of the red wine sauce on a plate and fan the chicken breast slices on the sauce.

If the skillet does not have an ovenproof handle, wrap the handle with a layer of aluminum foil.

Saskatoon-Basil Chicken Breasts with Saskatoon Chutney

In this recipe, saskatoon berries are mixed with rhubarb or cranberries to create a delicious chutney, and with red wine vinegar to create a fragrant basil marinade. You can substitute blueberries for the saskatoon berries.

SERVES 6

6 boneless, skinless **chicken breasts**

2 large handfuls **fresh basil leaves**

5 cloves **garlic**, peeled

1/4 cup (60 mL) **vegetable oil**

1/4 cup (60 mL) **olive oil**

1/4 cup (60 mL) **red wine vinegar**

finely grated **zest of 1 lemon**

1 cup (250 mL) **saskatoon berries**, or blueberries, fresh, or frozen and thawed

salt and **pepper**, to taste

Cut chicken breasts into 1 1/2-inch (4 cm) wide strips or leave whole.

In a food processor bowl, combine basil leaves, garlic, vegetable oil, olive oil, red wine vinegar, lemon zest, and saskatoon berries. Process until fairly smooth. Transfer the pesto to a large zip-lock bag and add the chicken. Seal the bag and toss to coat the chicken. Refrigerate six hours or overnight.

Preheat barbeque to medium heat. Oil the grill and barbeque the chicken until tender and just cooked. Remove from the grill and let rest, loosely covered, for 10 minutes. Serve with the Saskatoon Chutney.

Saskatoon Chutney

2 tsp (10 mL) **vegetable oil**

1/4 of a **red onion**, cut into thin strips

1 small clove **garlic**, minced

2 cups (500 mL) **saskatoon berries**, or blueberries, fresh, or frozen and thawed

1/2 cup (125 mL) cut-up **rhubarb**, or whole cranberries or lingonberries

1/4 cup (60 mL) **brown sugar**

1 tbsp (15 mL) **balsamic vinegar**

1 tsp (5 mL) **cornstarch** mixed with 1 tsp (5 mL) **water**

salt and **pepper**, to taste

In a medium saucepan over medium heat, sauté the onion and garlic in the oil. Add the saskatoon berries, rhubarb, brown sugar, and balsamic vinegar. Bring to a boil. Lightly mash the berries with a potato masher. Cook several minutes. Add the cornstarch/water mixture and stir until thickened slightly; season with salt and pepper. Cool and refrigerate until ready to serve.

Beer and Molasses Marinated Flank Steak

Dark beer is key to the success of this recipe. Serve this versatile steak as part of a main course with grilled vegetables and baby potatoes, warm on a bun, or cold atop a main dish salad.

SERVES 4 TO 6

2 lbs (907 g) **flank steak**, top sirloin, or round, trimmed

15 oz (440 mL) **dark beer**, such as Guinness

2 tbsp (30 mL) **molasses**

2 tbsp (30 mL) **Dijon mustard**

1 small **onion**, halved and sliced crosswise

3 cloves **garlic**, sliced

1 tsp (5 mL) **black pepper**

2 tbsp (30 mL) **olive oil**

2 tbsp (30 mL) **tomato paste**

To make the marinade, combine the beer, molasses, Dijon mustard, onion, garlic, black pepper, olive oil, and tomato paste in a medium bowl and whisk well.

Place the flank steak inside a plastic zip-lock bag and add the marinade. Seal and toss to coat the steak. Refrigerate overnight.

Preheat barbeque. Over medium heat, grill the steak, turning once, for about 5 to 7 minutes per side for medium rare.

Remove to a plate. Drape with a sheet of waxed paper and cover with a tea towel. Let rest 10 minutes.

Using a long slicing knife, slice the steak thinly on the diagonal across the grain. Serve warm or cold.

Rob's Southern Barbeque-Style Pulled Pork

Rob Reinhardt of Prairie Smoke and Spice does a mean pulled pork. As a certified Pacific Northwest Barbeque Association judge, I've judged his pork butt, as well as his ribs, brisket, and chicken at many competitions. Over the years he's perfected his low-and-slow hardwood-smoked recipes, and he and his team regularly win on the barbeque circuit. In 2010, he was named Canadian National Barbeque Champion. Not bad for a guy from the little village of Pilot Butte. Rob's winning rub is top secret, but here is his method for smoking pork butt, along with the recipe for one of his all-purpose rubs.

SERVES A CROWD

ROB'S ALL-PURPOSE RUB

1/3 cup (80 mL) **brown sugar**	2 tbsp (30 mL) **black pepper**
1/3 cup (80 mL) **seasoned salt**	2 tbsp (30 mL) **paprika**
3 tbsp (45 mL) **chili powder**	2 tsp (10 mL) **celery seed**
3 tbsp (45 mL) **granulated garlic** or garlic powder	1 tsp (5 mL) **cayenne powder**
	1 tsp (5 mL) **allspice**

one 7 to 9 lbs (3 to 4 kg) **whole pork butt**, also known as shoulder blade roast	**smoker**
	wood chunks, chips, or pellets
1/2 cup (125 mL) **yellow ballpark mustard**	wide heavy-duty **aluminum foil**
2 cups (500 mL) **apple juice**	digital probe (meat) **thermometer**

Classic Pulled Pork Sandwich

Between two Kaiser buns, pile a mound of pulled pork and a scoop of classic coleslaw. The textural contrast makes for a fantastic sandwich.

Smoking Tips

Pulled pork can be cooked on any smoker: electric, charcoal, or wood pellet. You can use any hardwood: apple, oak, hickory, and cherry are classic smoke flavours.

If you don't have a smoker, you can replicate the process on a gas grill that is capable of indirect heat. Place the meat on one side of the grill with no burners running under the meat. Place an aluminum pan

(CONTINUED ON PAGE 75)

Make the rub by combining the brown sugar, seasoned salt, chili powder, granulated garlic, black pepper, paprika, celery seed, cayenne powder, and allspice in a bowl. Stir well and set aside.

Trim the excess fat from roast. This cut is the upper portion of the front shoulder. You can choose bone-in or boneless, but if the bone is trimmed out, the roast will need to be tied closed. This is a cut that contains fat and collagen, the connective tissue that breaks down over the long cooking process, making the meat tender, sweet, and juicy. The pork butt is marbled with plenty of internal fat to keep the meat moist. Watch for veins and bone fragments and trim these away as well.

Smear the butt with a light coating of mustard. This will help the rub adhere and give you a better "bark" (the crispy exterior layer) on the finished pork. You will not be able to taste the mustard in the finished product.

Apply the spice rub at least thirty minutes and up to one day before you begin to cook the pork. Apply by coating the meat heavily, then press the rub into the meat with your hand. Sprinkle another light coat of rub on the meat just prior to placing it on the smoker.

Plan for a total cook and rest period of 1 1/2 hours per pound (1 1/2 hours per 454 g) at a temperature of 250°F (120°C). It will take roughly eleven to twelve hours to properly cook the meat.

Place the meat directly on a pre-heated smoker grate. Close the lid. Monitor the cooker temperature, but don't peek, as you will lose valuable heat. Flip and rotate the meat halfway through the cooking process. The meat is ready to come off the smoker when the internal temperature registers about 195°F to 200°F (90°C to 93°C) and the meat is very tender. The bone should pull cleanly out of the meat.

When the meat has reached the correct internal temperature, remove the pork to a tray and bring it inside for "hot holding."

Tear off a sheet of wide, heavy-duty foil about 28 inches (71 cm) long. Place the pork on one end of the sheet. Form a "boat" around the roast with the foil to prevent any juice from spilling out and pour the apple juice on the pork. Wrap the pork, taking care not to puncture the foil. You can add a second layer of foil if you wish. Once the pork is secure in the foil, wrap the package with a couple of old bath or beach towels to keep it insulated. You can transfer this bundle to a small picnic cooler with a lid. You can also place the bundle in a microwave but place a large tray under the roast to catch any juices that may leak out.

Let the meat rest for several hours to allow the pork to tenderize further and to allow the juice to pick up the smoky, spicy flavours of the "bark" on your pork. If your schedule does not allow for this resting period, just rest the finished roast on a cutting board for thirty minutes covered with a sheet of foil.

About 15 minutes before serving, unwrap the pork; reserve any juices. Using your hands, "pull" the pork into large chunks. Place the meat on a cutting board or in a pan, then shred the pork into small thumb-size pieces using two forks or your hands. (Vinyl gloves help.) Discard any large fat deposits that remain in the pork. If you have saved the juice from the foil, pour it over the pulled pork to add a lot more flavour. Serve and dig in!

Smoking Tips
(CONTINUED)

underneath the meat to catch the drippings. The burner on the opposite side of the grill should be on. You can place a foil-wrapped bundle of wood chips over the burner to generate smoke flavour, but be prepared to replace this bundle once per hour for the first four hours.

If you are monitoring the internal temperature, you will notice a long plateau of three to six hours at the 150°F to 165°F (66°C to 74°C) range. This is normal. During this period, the collagen (connective tissue) is being broken down into gelatin. This is the process that makes real barbeque so special.

Smoked Steelhead Trout

In this recipe, the steelhead trout is warm-smoked. Because it's an oily fish, it lends itself well to long, slow smoking. Don't be deterred by the length of time this fish smokes, which is one hour. The result is incredibly moist and tender. The rub recipe is a basic recipe to get you started. Add more or less of any ingredient to personalize it to your taste. For maximum flavour, be sure to use the freshest spices possible.

SERVES 4 TO 6

1 large **steelhead trout** or salmon fillet, skin on, about 1 ½ lbs (680 g)

vegetable oil, for brushing

SPICE RUB

2 tbsp (30 mL) **paprika powder**

2 tbsp (30 mL) **ground black pepper**

2 tbsp (30 mL) **granulated sugar**

2 tbsp (30 mL) **chili powder**

1 tbsp (15 mL) **garlic powder**

1 tbsp (15 mL) **onion powder**

1 tbsp (15 mL) **salt**

GLAZE

1 tbsp (15 mL) **liquid honey**

1 tbsp (15 mL) **soy sauce**

1 clove **garlic**, peeled and minced

1 tsp (5 mL) **Asian sesame oil**

To make the spice rub, in a small bowl, combine the paprika, black pepper, granulated sugar, chili powder, garlic powder, onion powder, and salt. Mix well. Set aside.

To make the glaze, in a medium bowl, whisk together the liquid honey, soy sauce, garlic, and sesame oil. Set aside.

Preheat smoker to 300°F (150°C).

Rinse the fish and pat it dry with a paper towel. With the skin side down and the flesh side up, brush the fillet with the oil. Sprinkle the rub liberally over the fillet to coat. Let stand about 10 minutes, during which time the rub will become moist.

When the smoker has come up to the required temperature, slide the fish with the skin side down onto the hot grate. Close the smoker lid, set the smoker to "smoke" mode, and smoke for about 15 minutes.

Set the temperature to about 220°F (105°C) to 250°F (120°C) and continue to cook for about 30 minutes. Open the smoker lid, and very gently brush or drizzle on the glaze. Close the lid and cook for another 15 minutes.

Slide the fillet onto a serving platter. Serve warm.

Chili-Rubbed Steelhead Trout

This zippy dish is big on flavour thanks to a pungent dry rub. I've provided instructions to prepare the fish on the stove, on a gas barbeque, or in a smoker. Leftovers are delicious made into a sandwich filling or added to a main dish salad.

SERVES 4 TO 6

SPICE RUB

1 tbsp (15 mL) **brown sugar**	1 tsp (5 mL) **salt**
1 tsp (5 mL) **ground cumin**	$^1/_2$ tsp (2 mL) **garlic powder**
1 tsp (5 mL) **chili powder**	$^1/_2$ tsp (2 mL) **onion powder**

prepared mustard, for brushing	1 large boneless **steelhead trout** or salmon fillet, skin on, about 1 $^1/_2$ lbs (680 g)

To make the spice rub, combine the brown sugar, ground cumin, chili powder, salt, garlic powder, and onion powder in a small bowl. Mix well. Set aside.

Rinse the fish and pat it dry with a paper towel. Lay the steelhead trout on a cutting board, skin side down. Brush the fillet with prepared mustard to coat. Sprinkle liberally with the spice rub.

STOVETOP METHOD: Cut the fillet into individual servings. Heat 1 tbsp (15 mL) vegetable oil in a medium-hot pan. Sear the fillets skin side up and flesh side down for 3 to 5 minutes. Turn the fillets and finish cooking, another 3 to 5 minutes.

GAS BARBEQUE METHOD: Cut the fillet into individual servings. Place each fillet, skin side up and flesh side down on a preheated, oiled hot grill. Close the barbeque lid and grill about 3 to 5 minutes over medium heat. Open the lid, turn the fillets, close lid, and finish grilling for another 3 minutes.

SMOKER METHOD: Leave the steelhead trout fillet whole. Preheat the smoker as per manufacturer's instructions. Place the fillet, skin side down and flesh side up, directly onto the grates. Close the lid and set the smoker to "smoke" mode for 15 minutes. Turn heat to 220°F (105°C) to 250°F (120°C), and let cook for another 45 minutes.

Sun-Dried Tomato and Ricotta Lasagne

This is a superb vegetarian lasagne that even meat lovers will enjoy.

SERVES 6

FRESH TOMATO SAUCE

1 can (28 oz/796 mL) **diced tomatoes** (not puréed tomatoes)

1 clove **garlic**, peeled and minced

1 tbsp (15 mL) **olive oil**

2 tbsp (30 mL) chopped **fresh basil**, or 2 tsp (10 mL) dried basil

¹/₂ tsp (2 mL) **chili flakes**

¹/₂ tsp (2 mL) **dried oregano**

salt and **pepper**, to taste

Purée the diced tomatoes in a blender or food processor. Transfer to a medium bowl and add the garlic, olive oil, fresh basil, chili flakes, and dried oregano. Stir well. Season with salt and pepper.

SUN-DRIED TOMATO AND RICOTTA FILLING

¹/₄ cup (60 mL) **sun-dried tomatoes** packed in oil

1 tbsp (15 mL) **capers**

¹/₂ tsp (2 mL) **dried oregano**

¹/₄ cup (60 mL) **pine nuts**, lightly toasted

¹/₂ cup (125 mL) grated **fresh Parmesan cheese** (do not use canned or pre-shredded cheese)

1 clove **garlic**, peeled and minced

5 oz (140 g) **garlic-and-fine-herb soft cheese**, such as Boursin brand

1 cup (250 mL) **regular** or light **ricotta cheese**

2 tbsp (30 mL) chopped **fresh basil**

salt and **pepper**, to taste

Roughly chop the sun-dried tomatoes and capers. In a medium bowl, combine the chopped tomatoes and capers, dried oregano, toasted pine nuts, grated Parmesan cheese, garlic, garlic-and-fine-herb soft cheese, ricotta cheese, and fresh basil. Mash and stir well. Season with salt and pepper.

A dragonfly perches atop oregano flowers in my garden.

LASAGNE

13 oz (370 g) **lasagne noodles**

Fresh Tomato Sauce

Sun-Dried Tomato and Ricotta Filling

12 oz (340 g) grated **mozzarella cheese**

14 oz (400 g) **fresh mushrooms**, sliced

2 tbsp (30 mL) **butter**

$^1/_2$ tsp (2 mL) **dried thyme leaves**

2 tsp (10 mL) **Worcestershire sauce**

salt and **pepper**, to taste

Preheat oven to 375°F (190°C).

Oil a standard 9- × 13- × 2-inch (3.5 L) (or equivalent) lasagne dish. Ladle a small amount of fresh tomato sauce just to cover the bottom of the dish. Cover with a single layer of lasagne noodles; trim the noodles to fit the dish. Spread the noodles with half the ricotta mixture. Top with $^1/_3$ of the tomato sauce. Sprinkle with a small amount of mozzarella cheese. Top with a layer of noodles followed by the remaining ricotta mixture, $^1/_3$ of the tomato sauce, and a sprinkling of mozzarella cheese. Top with another layer of noodles. Ladle the remaining tomato sauce on top and spread to cover. Top with the rest of the mozzarella cheese.

Cover the dish with lightly oiled foil.

Bake for 30 minutes. Remove the foil; bake another 20 to 30 minutes. Remove from the oven and let stand for 10 minutes before cutting.

Meanwhile, sauté the mushrooms in the butter. Cook, stirring occasionally until all the liquid has evaporated. Season with dried thyme, Worcestershire sauce, salt, and pepper.

To serve, cut the lasagne into individual portions and top each serving with the sautéed mushrooms.

Pasta with Feta Cheese, Fresh Tomatoes, and Basil

This is a super-quick dish that recalls a fragrant summer garden. Serve with a side salad for a quick and easy meal.

SERVES 4

11 oz (300 g) **pasta**,
such as linguine or spaghetti,
fresh or dried

2 tsp (10 mL) **kosher salt**

4 **vine-ripened tomatoes**,
halved and de-seeded

7 oz (200 g) soft, good quality
feta cheese or chèvre (goat cheese)

a good handful of **fresh basil leaves**

1/2 cup (125 mL) **garlic-infused olive oil**

Bring a large Dutch oven or stockpot two-thirds full of water to a boil. Add salt, and cook the pasta according to package directions, usually about 3 to 4 minutes for fresh pasta, or about 10 minutes for dried.

Meanwhile, deseed and chop the tomatoes. Crumble the feta cheese into medium chunks. Thinly slice the basil leaves.

Drain the pasta and return it to the empty pot. Pour the garlic oil over the pasta and add the tomatoes, feta cheese, and basil. Toss well and serve.

Spinach and Mushroom Quiche

This is a wonderful summertime brunch recipe. You can make and bake the quiche ahead of time and either freeze it or reheat it before serving.

SERVES 6 TO 8 / MAKES ONE 9-INCH (23 CM) QUICHE

2 tbsp (30 mL) **unsalted butter**

3 cups (750 mL) chopped **mushrooms**, such as button, cremini, chanterelles, morels, or a mixture

10 oz (280 g) **cooked spinach**, squeezed dry and chopped

$^1/_3$ cup (80 mL) finely diced **red pepper**

1 clove **garlic**, peeled and minced

salt and **pepper**

2 **green onions**, thinly sliced

6 **eggs**

1 cup (250 mL) **half-and-half cream**

One 9-inch (23 cm) **pie shell**, fully baked

4 $^1/_2$ oz (128 g) **blue cheese**, such as Danish, Stilton, or Roquefort, crumbled

Freshly gathered eggs at Farmgate Food, Balgonie, SK.

Preheat oven to 375°F (190°C).

In a large skillet, sauté the mushrooms in the butter until all the liquid has evaporated. Add the spinach, red pepper, and garlic. Stir for several minutes to heat through; season with salt and pepper. Spoon the mixture into the baked pie shell. Sprinkle with green onions.

In a medium bowl, whisk the eggs with a fork. Whisk in the cream; season with salt and pepper. Pour over the spinach-mushroom mixture and top with crumbled blue cheese.

Bake for about 35 minutes, or until a knife inserted into the middle comes out clean.

Serve with sliced garden-fresh tomatoes drizzled with a little olive oil and salt, or a side salad of baby greens tossed with a simple vinaigrette.

White Chocolate Berry Semifreddo

This is a lovely dessert to serve to company. The addition of the ricotta and tofu make it surprisingly low calorie. Haskap is a relatively new berry in Saskatchewan that works beautifully in this dessert, but any berry is delicious.

SERVES ABOUT 8 / MAKES TWO 5 $^{1}/_{2}$- × 3-INCH (500 ML) MINI LOAF PANS

1 $^{1}/_{2}$ cups (375 mL) **whipping cream**

$^{1}/_{2}$ cup (125 mL) **ricotta cheese**

10 $^{1}/_{2}$ oz (300 g) **silken** (soft) **tofu**, unflavoured

$^{3}/_{4}$ cup (185 mL) **granulated sugar**

$^{1}/_{4}$ tsp (1 mL) **almond extract**

$^{1}/_{2}$ cup (125 mL) chopped **white chocolate**

1 cup (250 mL) **frozen** or fresh **haskap berries**, raspberries, cranberries, or any other berry fruit

Lightly grease two 5 $^{1}/_{2}$- × 3-inch (500 mL) mini loaf pans. Line with plastic wrap, allowing the wrap to hang over the sides of the pans.

In a mixer bowl, beat the whipping cream to stiff peaks. Transfer to a medium bowl and set aside.

Using the same mixing bowl and the whisk attachment, beat the ricotta cheese and the tofu together with the granulated sugar and the almond extract until well mixed, about 1 minute.

Transfer the mixture to a fine mesh sieve. Sieve the mixture directly into the bowl with the whipped cream. (This is an important step as it breaks down the ricotta to create a silky texture.) Gently fold the ricotta-tofu mixture into the whipped cream.

Fold in the chopped white chocolate and the berries, being careful not to overfold or the fruit juices will run. Transfer the mixture to the loaf pans. Fold the plastic wrap over the mixture and freeze at least 3 hours, or overnight.

To serve, remove the semifreddo from the freezer about 30 minutes before serving to temper. Peel back the plastic wrap and remove the frozen loaf. Using a sharp knife (first run it under very hot water and dry the blade), slice the loaf into $^{1}/_{2}$-inch (1.5 cm) thick slices. Serve with additional fresh or frozen berries.

WHITE CHOCOLATE-BERRY/DARK CHOCOLATE-ALMOND VARIATION: After folding the ricotta-tofu mixture into the whipped cream, divide the semifreddo into two equal portions. Into one portion, gently fold in $^{1}/_{4}$ cup (60 mL) chopped white chocolate and $^{1}/_{2}$ cup (125 mL) frozen berries. Into the second portion, fold in $^{1}/_{4}$ cup (60 mL) chopped dark chocolate and $^{1}/_{2}$ cup (125 mL) whole almonds. Spread a layer of the berry mixture into the prepared pan, then a layer of the almond mixture, followed by the berry mixture and ending with the almond mixture. Freeze several hours before serving.

Dark Chocolate Cherry Brownies

Brownies and cherries—a wicked combination! How can anyone resist? Feel free to eat these "naked"...or "dress them up" with a fruit coulis and whipped cream. They are also excellent made with fresh raspberries.

MAKES ONE 8-INCH (20 CM) SQUARE CAKE

Carmine Jewel sour cherries at Over the Hill Orchards, Lumsden, SK.

³/₄ cup (185 mL) chopped 70% or 80% **dark chocolate**

¹/₂ cup (125 mL) **unsalted butter**

1 tsp (5 mL) **pure vanilla extract**

²/₃ cup (160 mL) **unbleached all-purpose flour**

3 tbsp (45 mL) **cocoa powder**, sifted

2 tsp (10 mL) **baking powder**

¹/₄ tsp (1 mL) **baking soda**

¹/₄ tsp (1 mL) **kosher salt**

2 **eggs**

³/₄ cup (185 mL) packed **brown sugar**

1 cup (250 mL) pitted and halved **sour cherries**, or whole fresh raspberries

Preheat oven to 350°F (180°C). Grease an 8-inch (20 cm) square baking pan.

In large glass measuring cup, combine the chopped chocolate and butter; microwave on high for 1 minute. Stir until the chocolate is completely melted. Add vanilla, and set aside to cool slightly.

Scoop the flour gently into measuring cups. Level the top with the flat edge of a knife and transfer the flour to a medium bowl. Add the sifted cocoa powder, baking powder, baking soda, and salt. Set aside.

In a large bowl, beat the eggs and brown sugar until thick and light, about 3 minutes. With a spatula, gently stir the flour mixture into egg mixture until just combined. Fold in the melted chocolate. Spread the batter into the prepared pan. Sprinkle with the cherries or fresh raspberries. Do not stir them into the batter.

Bake for 25 minutes, or until a cake tester inserted into the centre comes out with a very small amount of batter on it. Cool completely.

Basic Flaky Pastry (Pâte Brisée)

This is is my version of basic pastry, made with a combination of cold butter and frozen shortening.

MAKES ONE 9-INCH (23 CM) DOUBLE-CRUST PIE OR TWO 9-INCH (23 CM) SINGLE-CRUST PIE SHELLS

3 cups (750 mL) **unbleached all-purpose flour**

1 tsp (5 mL) **kosher salt**

²/₃ cup (160 mL) **frozen all-vegetable shortening** or lard

¹/₃ cup (80 mL) **cold butter**

about 1 cup (250 mL) **ice water**

In a large bowl, combine the flour and salt; mix well. Use a box grater to grate in the shortening and butter. Sweep up some of the flour with the fat as you grate.

Gather up some of the flour-fat mixture between your palms and rub with the heel of one hand in a downward motion once. Repeat 10 times, gathering up the flour-fat mixture each time.

Use a fork to mix in about ³/₄ cup (185 mL) ice water. Continue to add water in small amounts until the mixture feels slightly moist and begins to stick together.

Roll out the pastry as required.

Pastry-Making Tip

The method I use to make basic pie dough is a variation on the classic French "fraisage" method, where dough is smeared across the counter to incorporate the fat into the flour. In my method, handfuls of dough are gathered up into your hands, and the heel, not the palm, of one hand firmly "smears" the dough in a downward motion against the open palm of the other hand. Do this about 10 times. This action emulsifies some of the fat into the dough and leaves larger pieces of fat to create a very flaky crust.

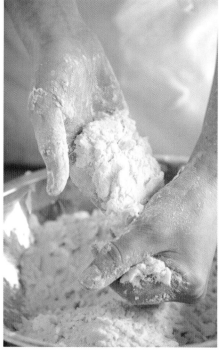

FOR A 9-INCH (23 CM) DOUBLE-CRUST SWEET OR SAVOURY PIE

Divide the dough in two and form each half into a ball. On a well-floured surface, flatten one ball slightly with your hands to create a disc. Sprinkle with flour. Using a floured rolling pin, roll out the pastry, being careful not to pull or tug the pastry. Do not turn the pastry over as this stretches the dough and will cause shrinkage when the crust bakes. Instead, gently lift the edges of the crust and sprinkle the counter under the crust with additional flour to keep the dough from sticking. Roll out the pastry to an 11-inch (28 cm) circle.

Fold the pastry in half and then in half again to create a triangle. Place the folded point of the pastry in the centre of a 9-inch (23 cm) pie plate. Gently unfold the crust, easing the pastry into place and being careful not to stretch the dough. Repair any tears with additional dough. Trim around the edge of the pie plate with a knife or the edge of a metal spatula.

Using the same technique, roll out the top crust to a 10-inch (25.5 cm) circle and fold it into a triangle. Gently place it inside the lined pie plate. Refrigerate for 30 minutes. Chilling the crust creates a flaky crust and prevents it from shrinking when baked.

Remove the chilled pastry from the refrigerator. Remove the top crust. Fill as required with a savoury or sweet filling. Unfold the top crust over the filling. Using a pair of kitchen scissors, trim the top crust to ½ inch (1.5 cm) beyond the edge of the bottom crust. Tuck top crust under the edge of the bottom pastry edge. Seal edges with your fingers. Make several slits in the top crust to allow steam to escape. Brush with beaten egg. If making a sweet pie, sprinkle the brushed top with a little granulated sugar.

Bake for 15 minutes at 425°F (220°C) and then reduce the temperature to 350°F (180°C) for another 35 minutes.

FOR TWO SINGLE 9-INCH (23 CM) CRUST PIE SHELLS

Divide the dough in two and form each half into a ball. On a well-floured surface, flatten one ball slightly with your hands to create a disc. Sprinkle with flour. Using a floured rolling pin, roll out the pastry, being careful not to pull or tug the pastry. Do not turn the pastry over as this stretches the dough and will cause shrinkage when the crust bakes. Instead, gently lift the edges of the crust and sprinkle the counter with additional flour under the crust to keep the dough from sticking. Roll out the pastry to an 11-inch (28 cm) circle.

Fold the pastry in half and then in half again to create a triangle. Place the folded point of the pastry in the centre of a 9-inch (23 cm) pie plate. Gently unfold, easing the pastry into place and being careful not to stretch the dough. Repair any tears with additional dough. Trim the edge of the crust to ½ inch (1.5 cm) beyond the edge of the pie plate. Fold the edge under the pastry (not the pie plate) and crimp with your fingers to create an attractive edge. Trim around the edge of the pie plate using a knife or the edge of a metal spatula. Repeat with the second ball.

Refrigerate both pie shells for 30 minutes to relax the dough. Chilling the crust creates a flaky crust, and prevents it from shrinking when it is baked.

The pie shells can be frozen at this point for later use.

For Partially or Fully Baked Pie Shells

Remove the prepared single crust pie shells from the refrigerator and prick the bottom and sides all over with a fork. This will release any steam that develops under the crust as it bakes.

For partially baked pie shells, bake the pie shell for about 15 to 20 minutes at 425°F (220°C).

For fully baked pie shells, bake the pie shells for about 25 to 30 minutes at 425°F (220°C).

Perfect Peach and Blueberry Lattice Pie

Peaches rank among my favourite fruits, and one reason is their versatility: they are delicious in jams, salsas, chutneys, and, of course, pies. Here, they pair with blueberries from the northern reaches of the Prairies.

MAKES ONE 9-INCH (23 CM) LATTICE-TOPPED PIE

1 recipe double-crust **Basic Flaky Pastry** (recipe on page 86)

6 medium, or 8 small, ripe **peaches**

3 tbsp (45 mL) **unbleached all-purpose flour**

1/2 tsp (2 mL) **kosher salt**

1 cup (250 mL) **granulated sugar**

1/2 cup (125 mL) **regular sour cream**

3/4 cup (185 mL) **fresh blueberries**

1/4 tsp (1 mL) **ground cinnamon**

1 tbsp (15 mL) **granulated sugar**

1 **egg**, beaten

1 tbsp (15 mL) **granulated sugar**

Preheat oven to 425°F (220°C).

Prepare the pastry dough as directed on page 86. Ease the crust into a 9-inch (23 cm) flan pan with removable bottom, or a shallow pie plate. Roll out the top crust to an 11-inch (28 cm) circle. Fold it and place it in the flan pan. Chill until ready to use. Do not prick the bottom of the crust.

To skin peaches, set the peaches in a large, heat-proof bowl. Pour boiling water over the peaches. Let stand 30 seconds. Drain and cover with cold water. After several seconds, the skins should begin to slip off very easily.

Using a sharp knife, cut each peach into 3/8-inch (1 cm) wide slices; discard the pit.

In a large bowl, combine the sliced peaches, flour, salt, and sugar. Stir to combine. Add the sour cream. Set aside.

Remove the chilled crust from the refrigerator. Remove the top crust. Add the peach filling. Scatter the blueberries over the filling.

In a small bowl, combine 1/4 tsp (1 mL) cinnamon with 1 tbsp (15 mL) granulated sugar. Stir well. Sprinkle over the top of filling.

To make the lattice top, unfold the top crust onto a lightly floured counter. Using a knife or fluted pastry wheel, cut it into 10 to 12 strips 3/4-inch (2 cm) wide. Working from top to bottom (lengthwise) on the flan pan, lay out 5 to 6 parallel strips on the top of the pie filling. Leave about a 1/2-inch (1.5 cm) space between each strip. Working from left to right (crosswise), weave one strip at a time over-and-under each lengthwise strip. Continue weaving the strips until all the pastry strips are used and a basket weave look has been accomplished. Trim the edges, and seal. Brush the lattice crust with beaten egg. Sprinkle the crust with 1 tbsp (15 mL) granulated sugar.

Bake at 425°F (220°C) for 15 minutes, then reduce heat to 350°F (180°C) and bake for an additional 35 minutes. Cool on a wire rack.

Sour Cherry Pie

I adore sour cherries. I'm convinced that the Saskatchewan Romance-series cherries are the best in the world. They are intense in cherry flavour, have a gorgeous crimson colour, and are superb in a pie. Their colour is so red you won't even be tempted to use any red food colouring.

MAKES ONE 9-INCH (23 CM) PIE

1 recipe double-crust **Basic Flaky Pastry** (recipe on page 86)

6 cups (1.5 L) pitted **sour cherries**

$^1/_3$ cup (80 mL) **unbleached all-purpose flour**

$^1/_2$ cup (125 mL) **granulated sugar**

$^1/_4$ tsp (1 mL) **pure almond extract**

1 **egg**, beaten

pinch **salt**

1 tbsp (15 mL) **soft butter**

1 **egg**, beaten

granulated sugar, for sprinkling

Preheat oven to 425°F (220°C).

Prepare pastry dough as directed on page 86. Ease the pastry into a 9-inch (23 cm) pie plate. Roll out the top crust to an 11-inch (28 cm) circle. Fold it and place it in the pie plate. Chill until ready to use. Do not prick the bottom of the crust.

If the cherries are large, cut them in half.

In a large bowl, stir together the pitted sour cherries, flour, sugar, almond extract, beaten egg, and a pinch of salt.

Remove the prepared crust from the refrigerator. Remove the top crust and set aside. Add the sour cherry filling. Dot the filling with bits of the butter.

Unfold the top crust over the filling. Using a pair of kitchen scissors, trim the top crust to $^1/_2$ inch (1.5 cm) beyond the edge of the bottom crust. Tuck the top crust under the edge of the bottom pastry. Seal edges with your fingers. Make several slits in the top crust to allow steam to escape. Brush with beaten egg. Sprinkle the crust with 1 tbsp (15 mL) granulated sugar.

Bake at 425°F (220°C) for 15 minutes, then reduce heat to 350°F (180°C) and bake for an additional 35 minutes. Cool on a wire rack.

prairie fruit
A SWEET LOVE AFFAIR

The Prairies offer a cornucopia of highly nutritious wild berries: blueberries, lingonberries, chokecherries, raspberries, and rosehips. The saskatoon berry, also called the serviceberry, is well established in virtually every corner of the Prairies. Blueberry-like clusters burst forth in mid-June on fifteen-foot-tall bushes. Pick a handful and pop them into your mouth. The plump berries burst blueberry flavour mingled with delicious overtones of almonds.

In days gone by, dried saskatoon berries and other native wild berries were crushed to a powder and mixed with dried meat and fat to make pemmican, a high-energy food that sustained Aboriginal people, fur traders, and explorers during their winters and on long, inland journeys. Today, the saskatoon berry is still popular, as urban foragers every June trek to pick-your-own farms or to farmers' markets to purchase bucketfuls to make into thick jams and sweet pies, and to freeze for use throughout the winter in sweet and savoury dishes. Although saskatoons still grow wild

on the wide-open prairies, significant amounts are grown commercially in all three Prairie provinces: the greatest production is in Alberta, while the highest number of processors are in Saskatchewan. Demand for this little-known berry keeps growing. Health-conscious Europeans are discovering its high antioxidant levels; large juice processors are adding the saskatoon berry to their antioxidant juice blends.

In 1999, a new fruit burst onto the Saskatchewan fruit scene: the dark red Carmine Jewel sour cherry, a sour cherry lover's dream with a classic cherry flavour. Bred at the University of Saskatchewan, this beautiful cherry is the first variety able to withstand the near cryogenic winters on the Prairies, where temperatures can drop to -50°C. Since then, five more varieties of sour cherry trees have been developed. Were the developers romantics at heart? Who knows, but they named the new family of cherries The Romance Series, with varieties christened Romeo, Juliet, St. Valentine, Cupid, and Crimson Passion. This family of hardy cherries can now be found throughout the province.

The U of S team is also working on a new berry called haskap, which is showing even more potential than the fabulous sour cherry. The haskap is a native berry, although very rare in Saskatchewan. The province is currently a world leader in haskap breeding: it has the largest and most diverse collection of this crop, with seedlings from Japan and Russia, and from all over Canada. Among new fruit plantings in the province, the haskap plant is number one, an indication of this berry's tremendous potential.

Prairie fruit is one of nature's sweet treats. The region's saskatoon berries, sour cherries, and haskaps are bursting with high levels of vitamins, minerals, fibre, and phytochemical antioxidants, each one a delicious addition to a healthy table.

ABOVE LEFT: Strawberry patch, Very Berry Farm, White City, SK.

ABOVE RIGHT: Fruit farmer Dean Kreutzer of Over the Hill Orchards tends to his strawberries high up in the Lumsden Valley, SK.

Saskatoon Berries

Sour Cherries

Lingonberries

Strawberries

Raspberries

Blueberries

91

Cornmeal-Blueberry Muffins

This is a variation on the first muffin recipe I ever received. When I was about 14 years old I was enrolled in the Homemaker 4H course, where we learned about cooking and sewing. Two of my favourite recipes from that course were Apple Crisp and Blueberry Muffins. I've changed this recipe over the years to include cornmeal, lemon rind, and plain yogurt. Saskatoon berries and lingonberries also are delicious in these tasty muffins.

MAKES 1 DOZEN MUFFINS

Early morning sun shines on these blueberries, still covered with morning dew. Over the Hill Orchards, Lumsden, SK.

1 ³/₄ cups (435 mL) **unbleached all-purpose flour**

¹/₄ cup (60 mL) **cornmeal**

¹/₃ cup (80 mL) **granulated sugar**

2 ¹/₂ tsp (12 mL) **baking powder**

¹/₄ tsp (1 mL) **baking soda**

³/₄ tsp (3 mL) **kosher salt**

finely grated **rind of 1 lemon**

1 **egg**, lightly beaten

³/₄ cup (185 mL) **milk***

¹/₂ cup (125 mL) **plain yogurt***

¹/₃ cup (80 mL) **unsalted butter**, melted

1 ¹/₃ cups (330 mL) **blueberries** or saskatoon berries, fresh or frozen

Preheat oven to 400°F (200°C). Grease a 12-cup muffin tin, or line with paper muffin cups.

Combine flour, cornmeal, sugar, baking powder, baking soda, salt, and lemon rind in a large bowl. Stir to combine.

In a separate bowl whisk together the egg, milk, yogurt, and melted butter. Add to the dry ingredients. Mix until almost combined.

Fold in the blueberries. Do not over mix.

Scoop the batter into the prepared muffin pan (a large ice cream scoop works well).

Bake for 18 to 20 minutes. Remove the baked muffins from oven and let them rest in the pan for 10 minutes before removing them to a wire rack to cool.

*Milk and yogurt can be omitted and substituted with 1 ¹/₄ cups (300 mL) buttermilk.

Blueberry-Bran Muffins

A healthy way to start the day.

MAKES 12 LARGE MUFFINS

1 cup (250 mL) **bran cereal**, such as 100% Bran

$^1/_2$ cup (125 mL) **old-fashioned** or quick **rolled oats**

1 $^1/_3$ cups (330 mL) **milk**

$^1/_4$ cup (60 mL) **vegetable oil** or melted butter

1 **egg**, beaten with a fork

1 cup (250 mL) **whole wheat flour**

2 tsp (10 mL) **baking powder**

1 tsp (5 mL) **ground cinnamon**

$^1/_4$ tsp (1 mL) **salt**

$^1/_2$ cup (125 mL) **brown sugar**

1 $^1/_2$ cups (375 mL) **blueberries**, fresh or frozen

Preheat oven to 400°F (200°C). Grease a 12-cup muffin tin, or line with paper muffin cups. Set aside.

In a large bowl, combine the bran cereal and the rolled oats. Add the milk and the oil. Stir and let stand for 10 minutes. Whisk in the egg and mix well.

Meanwhile, in a medium bowl, combine the whole wheat flour, baking powder, ground cinnamon, salt, and brown sugar. Mix well. Add to the wet ingredients and stir only until a few traces of flour remain. Fold in the blueberries.

Using a large spoon or ice cream scoop, transfer the batter to the muffin tin. Bake for 18 to 20 minutes, or until a toothpick inserted into the centre comes out clean.

Serve warm or at room temperature.

Hutterite Yogurt

This method for making yogurt comes from my good friend Lydia Hofer, of Arm River Hutterite Colony outside Lumsden, Saskatchewan. This yogurt is clean-tasting and so thick you can literally stand a spoon in it. The trick is to drain the yogurt after it has set. This recipe can easily be halved if you wish to make a smaller quantity.

MAKES A LARGE BATCH

16 cups (4 L) **milk** (2% or 3.25% milk fat)

1 cup (250 mL) **plain yogurt** (2% or 3.25% milk fat) with active bacterial culture and no thickeners or fillers (this is essential)

an **instant-read thermometer** or candy thermometer

cheesecloth, to line a large colander

an **electric heating pad** or electric blanket

Yogurt-Making Tip

If you do not have a heating pad, an alternative is to pre-warm your oven to 200°F (93°C) and then turn it off. Using an oven thermometer to monitor temperature, check the temperature frequently to ensure that it does not drop below 100°F (38°C) but does not exceed 120°F (49°C). Too warm an oven will kill the active bacteria. Turn oven on for short periods during incubation to maintain a temperature of 108°F–112°F (42°C–44°C).

In a large Dutch oven or stockpot, scald the milk, then cool it quickly by placing the pot in the refrigerator (or outside in winter).

When the temperature of the milk has cooled to between 110°F and 115°F (43°C–46°C), skim off any skin that has formed on the top of the milk. Very gently, stir in 1 cup (250 mL) yogurt (vigorous mixing will incorporate too much air into the milk and slow down the setting process).

Cover the pot and place it on a heating pad set at medium temperature. Wrap as much of the heating pad as possible around the pot and then wrap the heating pad and pot in a blanket so that the pot is completely covered.

Let the mixture sit for approximately five hours with the temperature not exceeding 120°F (49°C) and not dropping below 100°F (38°C). (Check it from time to time with an instant-read thermometer or a candy thermometer.) The ideal temperature for making yogurt is about 108°F–112°F (42°C–44°C). Do not stir.

After approximately four hours, gently scoop the yogurt with a spoon; it should be thick and leave an indentation. If not, let the yogurt sit longer. Do not stir. Don't worry if it takes longer than five hours—just be patient.

Once the yogurt has set, refrigerate it overnight.

The next morning, transfer the yogurt to a colander lined with two layers of moistened cheesecloth. Leave the yogurt to drain for about two hours. (Depending on the size of your colander, you may have to do this process in several batches.)

Transfer the drained yogurt to containers and refrigerate. (You can rinse the cheesecloth and save it for the next time you make yogurt.)

This yogurt will keep for weeks in the refrigerator. When you need to make another batch, reserve 1 cup (250 mL) of the yogurt. It will be your starter.

Aspen's golden leaves dance in the prairie winds,

Maturing rays cast long shadows,

Pregnant stalks bend, heavy with wheat, flax, lentils,

Combines hum to gather in the harvest.

Hearty soups, rich stews,

Trees heavy with apples sweet to the core,

Squirrels busily stockpile their harvest, too...

The time of abundance.

The time of Thanksgiving.

A sure sign of fall is bales of hay topped with mountains of pumpkins. Lincoln Gardens, Lumsden, SK.

autumn

Roasted Butternut Squash Soup

Roasting the squash creates a deeply flavoured soup. To create a silky texture, be sure to sieve the soup to remove any seeds and vegetable bits.

SERVES 4 AS AN APPETIZER (DOUBLE THE RECIPE FOR A MAIN COURSE SOUP)

5 cups (1.25 L) peeled, seeded and diced **butternut squash**

1 **small leek**, white part only, halved lengthwise, root end discarded

1 **tomato**, halved

1 clove **garlic**, skin on

vegetable oil, for drizzling and oiling the pan

$1\frac{1}{2}$ tsp (7 mL) **dried thyme**

salt and **pepper**, to taste

3 cups (750 mL) **chicken** or vegetable **stock**, not water

$\frac{1}{2}$ cup (125 mL) **heavy** or light **cream**

1 to 2 tbsp (15 to 30 mL) chopped **fresh parsley** or chives for garnish

Preheat oven to 425°F (220°C).

Line a cookie sheet with aluminum foil and oil lightly. Spread diced butternut squash, leek halves, tomato halves, and garlic on the pan. Drizzle with oil, and sprinkle with dried thyme, salt, and pepper. Toss gently. Roast in the oven for about 30 minutes, removing the leek halves after about 15 minutes to avoid burning them.

Remove and discard the skin from the roasted garlic. Transfer vegetables and garlic to a food processor. Add about 1 cup (250 mL) stock; purée, and add more stock as necessary.

Sieve the soup through a fine mesh sieve or food mill into a clean pot. Return to the heat, and add the remaining stock. Reheat the soup without boiling. Add $\frac{1}{2}$ cup (125 mL) cream and additional stock, if required. Taste, and season with salt and pepper.

Ladle the soup into bowls and garnish with parsley or chives.

Curried Pumpkin and Coconut Soup

This recipe takes pumpkin up a notch with some exotic flair. Toasting the spices deepens their flavour to create a rich-tasting dish.

SERVES 4 TO 6

1 tbsp (15 mL) **vegetable oil**

1 **onion**, peeled and quartered

1 clove **garlic**

2 ¹/₂ tsp (12 mL) **curry powder**, or Indian-style curry paste

¹/₂ tsp (2 mL) **ground cumin**

¹/₂ tsp (2 mL) **ground turmeric**

¹/₄ tsp (1 mL) **ground cinnamon**

1 tsp (5 mL) grated **fresh ginger**

pinch **cayenne powder**

2 cups (500 mL) **chicken stock** or vegetable stock, not water

2 cups (500 mL) **puréed pumpkin** (Do not use pumpkin pie filling)

14 oz (400 mL) **coconut milk**, preferably full fat

toasted, unsalted pumpkin seeds, for garnish

In a food processor, finely chop the onion and garlic.

In a medium saucepan over medium-low heat, heat the oil. Add the onion-garlic mixture and lightly sauté without browning for about 5 minutes. Add the curry powder, cumin, turmeric, cinnamon, fresh ginger, and cayenne powder. Toast the spices, stirring constantly for 1 minute.

Add the stock and the pumpkin purée. Stir well and bring to a simmer. Simmer 5 to 10 minutes.

Add the coconut milk and heat through without letting the soup come to a boil. Season with salt and pepper, to taste.

Ladle the soup into bowls and garnish with toasted pumpkin seeds.

Sliced Beets with Warm Chèvre

In this recipe, the creamy goat cheese, also known as chèvre, pairs beautifully with the sweet and earthy flavour of roasted beets. Serve this delicious dish as an individual starter salad or on a large platter.

SERVES 4 TO 6

8 medium **fresh beets**, tops and bottom root ends removed, and peeled

olive oil, for drizzling

salt and **pepper**, for sprinkling

$^1/_2$ lb (250 g) log of **creamy chèvre** (goat cheese), sliced into $^3/_4$-inch (2 cm) thick rounds

1 **egg**

1 tbsp (15 mL) **water**

$^1/_2$ cup (125 mL) **ground hazelnuts** or walnuts

vegetable oil, for frying

1 tbsp (15 mL) **hazelnut** or walnut **oil**

2 tbsp (30 mL) **vegetable oil**

1 tbsp (15 mL) **cider** or malt **vinegar**

1 tsp (5 mL) **maple syrup**

salt and **pepper**, to taste

2 **oranges**

1 cup (250 mL) **arugula**, frisée lettuce, or pea shoots

Artisanal Cheesemaking

Artisanal cheese-making is an emerging industry in Saskatchewan. One of the very first cheese producers is SalayView Farms near Lang, SK. They make a lovely, mild, soft chèvre from the milk produced by their Nigerian Dwarf goats, pictured above.

BEETS: Preheat oven to 400°F (200°C). Place the whole prepared beets in a shallow oiled pan. Drizzle with olive oil and sprinkle with salt and pepper. Cover with foil and bake about 1 hour, or until fork tender. Cool slightly. Slice each beet into $^1/_2$-inch (1.5 cm) thick rounds. (The beets can be prepared in advance and gently reheated before serving.)

CHÈVRE: In a small bowl, whisk the egg with 1 tbsp (15 mL) water. Place the ground nuts in a separate small bowl. Dip each round of sliced chèvre into the egg mixture and then into the ground nuts. Turn to coat completely. Set aside. (The chèvre can be prepared to this point and refrigerated until ready to cook.) Preheat a large fry pan over medium heat. Pour in just enough oil to cover the bottom of the pan. Fry the nut-coated rounds until golden brown and heated completely through; the centre of each round should be soft to the touch.

DRESSING: Whisk together the hazelnut or walnut oil, 2 tbsp (30 mL) vegetable oil, cider or malt vinegar, maple syrup, and salt and pepper. Set aside. (The dressing can be prepared in advance.)

ORANGES FOR GARNISH: With a sharp paring knife, remove the rind from the oranges; make sure to remove all the bitter white pith. Carefully remove individual orange segments by sliding your paring knife on either side of each segment's membrane. Set aside. (The oranges can be prepared in advance and refrigerated until serving time.)

TO SERVE: Depending on the size of the beets, lay 3 to 5 beet rounds, each overlapping slightly, in the centre of an appetizer plate. Top the beets with 1 or 2 rounds of warm chèvre, then a small handful of arugula leaves. Top with several orange slices and a drizzle of the dressing.

Prairie Antipasto Platter

Instead of featuring the usual cured meats, give your antipasto platter some prairie flair with thinly sliced bison steak, pickled onions, marinated roasted red peppers, and slow-roasted tomatoes. Paired with some crusty bread and a glass of wine, this tapas party dish will delight and intrigue your guests.

SERVES 6

One 2 lb (1 kg) **round** or flank **bison steak**, trimmed

MARINADE

1 **chipotle pepper** with adobo sauce

1 large clove **garlic**, quartered

2 tbsp (30 mL) **extra virgin olive oil**

2 tbsp (30 mL) **balsamic vinegar**

1/2 tsp (2 mL) **ground cumin**

1 tsp (5 mL) coarsely ground **black pepper**

1/2 tsp (2 mL) **Hungarian paprika**

1 tbsp (15 mL) **fresh thyme leaves**

2 tsp (10 mL) **molasses**

Pickled Red Onions
(recipe on facing page)

Marinated Roasted Red Peppers
(recipe on facing page)

Slow-Roasted Tomatoes
(recipe on page 63)

In a small food processor bowl, process the chipotle pepper with adobo sauce, garlic, olive oil, balsamic vinegar, cumin, black pepper, paprika, thyme, and molasses to a coarse paste.

Place the steak in a large zip-lock bag. Add the marinade. Seal the bag and toss it to thoroughly coat the steak. Marinate overnight in the refrigerator. Remove steak from refrigerator 30 minutes before grilling.

Preheat barbeque.

Remove the meat from the bag and place it on the grill. Sear it on both sides over medium heat until rare to medium rare, about 5 to 7 minutes per side. Remove from the grill and transfer to a platter. Cover with a sheet of waxed paper and then with a tea towel. Let the meat rest for at least 10 minutes. If not serving immediately, refrigerate the meat until serving time. When ready to serve, slice the meat very thinly on the diagonal.

Serve on a large platter with the Pickled Red Onions, Marinated Roasted Red Peppers, and Slow-Roasted Tomatoes.

Marinated Roasted Red Peppers

5 large **red peppers**

MARINADE

¹/₄ cup (60 mL) finely chopped **fresh basil**

¹/₄ cup (60 mL) finely chopped **fresh oregano**

2 tbsp (30 mL) **fresh thyme leaves**

1 clove **garlic**, minced

5 tbsp (75 mL) **extra virgin olive oil**

2 tbsp (30 mL) **red wine vinegar**

2 tbsp (30 mL) **balsamic vinegar**

¹/₂ tsp (2 mL) **kosher salt**

¹/₄ tsp (1 mL) freshly ground **black pepper**

Preheat barbeque to high heat. Char peppers directly on the grill until black on all sides. Remove to a plate. Cut a slit in the peppers and let them sit until cool enough to handle. Peel off the charred outer skin. Discard the skin, stem, and seeds. Cut each pepper into bite-size pieces. Transfer to a bowl.

In a small bowl, whisk together the basil, oregano, thyme, garlic, olive oil, red wine vinegar, balsamic vinegar, salt, and pepper. Pour the marinade over the red peppers. Toss gently. Cover and refrigerate for several hours.

Pickled Red Onions

1 large **red onion**, peeled and thinly sliced

¹/₄ cup (60 mL) **granulated sugar**

¹/₂ cup (125 mL) **red wine vinegar**, or raspberry-flavoured red wine vinegar

1 **bay leaf**

5 **peppercorns**

pinch **kosher salt**

In a small saucepan, bring the granulated sugar, vinegar, bay leaf, peppercorns, and salt to a boil. Add the sliced red onion, pressing down to submerge as much of the onion as possible. Chill. Transfer the onion and liquid to a jar, seal, and refrigerate until ready to use.

Stuffed Mini Pumpkins

What a way to dress up Thanksgiving! I made these cute little pumpkins during the first season of *The Wheatland Café* in 2006. Florists across Saskatchewan had no idea what had happened when customers turned up asking to buy these tiny gourds, which are typically used as a table decoration. Since then, florist shops and grocery stores now carry unvarnished, mini pumpkins as a regular item in the fall. Inspired by a recipe I found many years ago, I've given these little pumpkins some prairie flair by adding nutty wild rice and a few other ingredients. This side dish is sure to bring you plenty of "oohs" and "aahs."

MAKES 10

10 **mini pumpkins**, unvarnished (do not purchase decorative gourds)

¼ cup (60 mL) **wild rice**, soaked overnight

¾ cup (185 mL) **water**

vegetable oil, for sautéing

1 **medium cooking onion**, finely chopped

1½ cups (375 mL) **green peas**

1 small or half a large **red pepper**, finely chopped

1¾ cups (435 mL) **corn kernels**, fresh or frozen

1 **jalapeño pepper**, seeded and finely chopped

1 tsp (5 mL) **chili powder**

½ tsp (2 mL) **ground cumin**

⅛ tsp (.5 mL) **ground coriander**

salt and **pepper**, to taste

Presoaking Wild Rice

The wild rice recipes in this cookbook were developed using wild rice that has been presoaked for at least four hours (or overnight) prior to cooking. Presoaking is particularly effective if you are cooking rice that is older than one year and has lost some of its moisture. The presoak ensures a more evenly cooked product and one that cooks up in less time than rice that has not been presoaked. Any of the recipes in this book can be prepared without presoaking the rice, but you may have to increase the liquid amount and extend the cooking time.

Preheat oven to 350°F (180°C).

Make a slit about ½-inch (1.5 cm) on either side of the stem of each pumpkin to allow steam to escape. Place the prepared pumpkins on a cookie sheet and bake, uncovered, for about 45 minutes, or until tender. Remove from the oven and let cool. (This step can be done in advance.)

To make the wild rice, drain the soaked rice and rinse. Bring ¾ cup (185 mL) water to a boil and add the soaked wild rice. Cover, and simmer on low heat for 45 minutes, or until the rice starts to puff. Remove from heat.

In a medium skillet, heat the oil to medium, and sauté the onion until translucent. Add the peas, and sauté until tender crisp. Add the red pepper, corn, cooked wild rice and jalapeño; stir to combine. Add the chili powder, cumin, ground coriander, salt and pepper. Remove from heat. (This step can be done in advance.)

Carefully cut a circle around the top of each pumpkin, about ½-inch (1.5 cm) from the stem. Remove top and trim off any seeds and stringy bits. Using a small spoon, scoop out the seeds and stringy bits from within each pumpkin. Fill the cavity with the vegetable mixture so that there is a small mound poking over the top. Replace the lid at a slight angle.

Bake at 350°F (180°C) for about 15 minutes.

These pumpkins can be prepared in advance and refrigerated. Remove from the refrigerator about 30 minutes before reheating. Heat the pumpkins at 350°F (180°C) until heated through, about 20 minutes.

Freshly picked mini pumpkins at Lincoln Gardens, Lumsden, SK.

105

Wild Rice-Stuffed Acorn Squash

Fall gardens burst with green acorn squash, fat orange pumpkins, bright red tomatoes, and yellow zucchini. This recipe is delicious as a vegetarian main course or with fish or chicken.

SERVES 4 TO 6

¹/₂ cup (125 mL) **wild rice**, soaked overnight

2 cups (500 mL) **water**

2 to 3 **acorn squash** (or your favourite squash variety)

7 oz (200 g) **button** or cremini **mushrooms**, chopped

1 tbsp (15 mL) **unsalted butter**

1 cooking **onion**, chopped

1 clove **garlic**, chopped

1 tsp (5 mL) **vegetable oil**

1 **Granny Smith apple**, peeled, cored, and chopped into ¹/₂-inch (1.5 cm) pieces

¹/₄ cup (60 mL) **dried cranberries**, or raisins

¹/₄ cup (60 mL) **pine nuts**

1 ¹/₂ tsp (7 mL) **dried thyme** or 1 ¹/₂ tbsp (22 mL) fresh thyme

salt and **pepper**, to taste

³/₄ cup (185 mL) grated **old cheddar cheese**

Preheat oven to 350°F (180°C).

Drain the wild rice and rinse. In a saucepan, bring the water to a boil. Add the rice, cover, and simmer until tender and just starting to puff, about 45 minutes. Drain, if necessary.

Meanwhile, cut the squash in half. Scrape out the seeds. Place cut side down on a parchment paper–lined cookie sheet and bake for 45 minutes, or until tender. Remove from the oven and let cool slightly.

In a medium skillet, sauté the mushrooms in the butter until they release their juices. Simmer until the juices disappear. Season with salt and pepper.

In a separate medium skillet, sauté the onion and garlic in the oil until translucent. Add the apple, and cook until tender. Sprinkle with the cranberries, pine nuts, thyme, salt, and pepper. Stir well. Add the cooked wild rice, and stir. Add the cooked mushrooms, and mix well.

Fill the cavity of each squash with the wild rice mixture. Sprinkle with cheddar cheese. Bake for 20 minutes, until heated through and the cheese has started to brown. Serve hot.

wild rice
AN ABORIGINAL DELICACY

It may surprise you that those nutty, slightly chewy, shiny black kernels that are so distinctly Canadian and so highly sought-after are not indigenous to the Prairies. Indeed, wild rice, the only native cereal crop in North America, is a water plant native to the Great Lakes. The grain has been spread geographically by humans, who have planted the water grass in various lake regions in Canada and the United States. Wild rice was introduced into the pristine waters of northern Saskatchewan in the mid-1930s to feed ducks, geese, muskrat, and moose, and to enhance hunting and trapping capabilities.

The species that is grown in Saskatchewan is *Zizania palustris*. Saskatchewan wild rice is grown organically, without chemicals or pesticides, and since the 1960s has become an important cash crop for northern communities. Today, northern Saskatchewan is the "rice bowl" of Canada and produces more than half of the country's wild rice crop. Its wild rice has gained a superb reputation for being a premium product.

Wild rice is pricey. It's finicky to grow. And it's labour intensive to harvest and process. Before wild rice can grace your plate, it must be picked. Traditionally, the grass was harvested by hand in a two-man canoe by Aboriginal people. Using tapered sticks, the rice heads would be knocked off the stalks into the bottom of the canoe. Some bands still harvest this way today, although airboat harvesters are now commonplace, with rice being collected into a large bucket known as a "speedhead" fastened to the front of the boat. Once harvested, the "green" rice is cured for five to ten days in windrows, where it is turned daily to ensure all the grains ripen evenly. In batches, it is transferred to parching ovens to bake, remove moisture, and give it that telltale toasty flavour. Rollers hull the rice to remove the chaff from the kernel and to expose the black shiny grains.

The grains are then cleaned, graded, and bagged. Only then is the product ready for shipping to buyers, supermarkets, and specialty shops across Canada, the United States, Asia, and Europe.

Wild rice is high in protein, carbohydrates, and minerals. It is low in fat and is a source of dietary fibre, B vitamins, and linoleic acid. A little goes a long way, as it triples and even quadruples in volume when cooked. It's delicious in just about any dish from soup, pilafs, and salads, to stuffings for fowl, and even desserts. Dress up a side dish of wild rice by preparing it with pine nuts, beef broth, and dried cranberries. Add a cupful of cooked wild rice to yeast dough for an interesting texture and flavour. Grind uncooked wild rice using a food processor or coffee grinder to produce a delicious-tasting gluten-free "flour." Be sure to purchase wild rice that has a fresh toasty aroma and unbroken, long, and shiny kernels.

107

Wild Rice and Chickpea Salad

This prairie salad is a tasty way to get in loads of fibre and to celebrate wild rice and chickpeas. My family can't get enough of this delicious dish.

SERVES 4 AS A MAIN COURSE

1 cup (250 mL) **wild rice**, soaked overnight

4 cups (1 L) **beef**, chicken, or vegetable **stock**

1 can (19 oz/540 mL) **chickpeas**, drained and rinsed

2 **fresh tomatoes**, deseeded and diced

1/2 cup (125 mL) sliced **white onion**

1/2 cup (125 mL) diced **English cucumber**

1/3 cup (80 mL) **dried cranberries**

1/3 cup (80 mL) **toasted pine nuts**, or toasted sliced almonds

1/4 cup (60 mL) chopped **dried apricots**

1/4 cup (60 mL) coarsely chopped **fresh mint leaves**

3 tbsp (45 mL) **vegetable oil**

2 tbsp (30 mL) **hazelnut oil***

3 tbsp (45 mL) **sherry vinegar** or red wine vinegar

2 tsp (10 mL) **honey** or maple syrup

1/2 tsp (2 mL) **Dijon mustard**

Drain the wild rice and rinse. In a medium saucepan, bring the stock to a boil, and add the wild rice. Reduce heat to a simmer, cover, and cook about 45 minutes, or until the rice begins to puff but is not totally soft and all liquid has been absorbed. Set aside to cool.

In a large salad bowl, combine the rinsed chickpeas, tomatoes, white onion, cucumber, dried cranberries, toasted pine nuts, dried apricots, and fresh mint. Add the cooled rice.

To make the dressing, in a small bowl, whisk together the vegetable oil, hazelnut oil, sherry vinegar, honey, and Dijon mustard. Pour over the salad and toss well.

Season with salt and pepper. Taste and adjust seasonings.

* Hazelnut oil is available in specialty food shops. If you can't find it, substitute walnut oil or additional vegetable oil.

Black Bean-Quinoa Salad

This is a power-packed salad. Quinoa is a complete protein, gluten-free, and a good source of fibre, complex carbs, and vitamins. Although still a minor crop on the prairies, quinoa is starting to find its way onto more and more dinner plates. Enjoy this amazing salad as a main course with a slice of Oatmeal-Raisin Bread (recipe on page 144) or as a side dish. Leftovers are delicious in your lunchbox.

SERVES 8

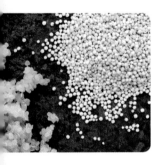

Cooked & uncooked quinoa.

³/₄ cup (185 mL) **quinoa**

1 ¹/₂ cups (375 mL) **water**

half a large **carrot**, finely chopped, or finely julienned, or shredded

2 **green onions**, sliced

half an **English cucumber**, seeded and diced

half a **sweet pepper**, red, yellow or green, diced

¹/₃ cup (80 mL) **toasted pine nuts**, or pumpkin seeds

1 can (19 oz/540 mL) **black beans**, drained and rinsed well

handful **fresh basil**, chopped

handful **fresh parsley**, chopped

¹/₃ cup (80 mL) **extra virgin olive oil**

2 tbsp (30 mL) **fresh lemon juice**

1 clove **garlic**, peeled and minced

salt and **pepper**, to taste

Place quinoa in a sieve and rinse under cold water for 3 minutes to remove any bitterness from the outer husk.

In a medium-sized pot with a lid, bring the water to a boil. Add the quinoa and simmer, covered, for about 20 to 25 minutes. Remove from the heat. Fluff the cooked quinoa with a fork. Let stand, uncovered, about 10 minutes, then spread out on a parchment paper–lined cookie sheet. Let sit until cool and slightly dry.

In a large bowl, combine the carrot, green onions, cucumber, pepper, toasted pine nuts, and black beans. Stir. Add the fresh basil, parsley, and the cooled quinoa. Stir gently to combine.

For the dressing, in a small bowl, whisk together the olive oil, fresh lemon juice, garlic, salt, and pepper. Pour over the salad and toss well. Taste and adjust seasonings.

Grilled or Roasted Cumin Carrots

The bold aromatic spices in this recipe toast as the carrots bake to create a deep, rich flavour. These can also be oven-roasted at 425°F (220°C) for 30 to 40 minutes.

SERVES 4

1 lb (454 g) **carrots**, peeled and cut on the diagonal into 2-inch (5 cm) wide chunks

2 tbsp (30 mL) **olive oil**

1 tsp (5 mL) *each* **ground cumin** and **ground coriander**

¹/₂ tsp (2 mL) **dried thyme** or Italian herb blend

1 tsp (5 mL) **coarse sea salt**

¹/₂ tsp (2 mL) **ground pepper**

Preheat barbeque to high. Preheat a vegetable grill basket in the barbeque with the lid down. In a plastic bag, toss together the oil, cumin, coriander, thyme, salt, and pepper. Add the carrots and toss well. Pour the contents of the bag into the preheated grill basket and grill with the lid down for about 30 minutes, stirring occasionally, until tender crisp. Serve hot.

Herb and Garlic Roasted Carrots

Your kitchen will be filled with the most incredible aroma as these carrots roast. Be sure to use fresh herbs. A sprig includes the main stem of the herb, plus the leaves.

SERVES 4

1 lb (454 g) **carrots**, peeled and cut into narrow sticks 3 inches (7.5 cm) long

olive oil, for drizzling

5 cloves of **garlic**, peeled and bruised slightly

4 large sprigs **fresh thyme**

1 large stalk **fresh rosemary**

coarse sea salt and **pepper**, to taste

1 tbsp (15 mL) finely chopped **fresh parsley**

Preheat oven to 425°F (220°C). Line a cookie sheet with parchment paper, or with aluminum foil. Set aside.

Place the carrots on the prepared cookie sheet. Drizzle with olive oil and add the cloves of garlic. Break the thyme and rosemary into pieces and scatter them over the carrots. Sprinkle the mixture with the coarse salt, and pepper. Toss the carrots with your hands to completely coat them with the oil.

Roast for about 30 minutes, stirring the carrots once. Transfer the roasted carrots to a serving platter and sprinkle with the parsley. Serve hot.

Carrots with Horseradish-Cream Sauce

This recipe from my childhood has a permanent spot in my recipe box. I love these carrots as a side dish to any meat, but the horseradish makes them especially good with roast beef.

SERVES 4 TO 6

4 cups (1 L) **carrots**, peeled and cut into narrow sticks about 3 inches (7.5 cm) long

¹/₂ cup (125 mL) **mayonnaise**

1 tbsp (15 mL) **minced onion**

1 tbsp (15 mL) **prepared horseradish**

salt and **pepper**, to taste

2 tbsp (30 mL) **dry breadcrumbs**

1 to 2 tbsp (15 to 30 mL) chopped **fresh parsley**

paprika, for sprinkling

1 tbsp (15 mL) **butter**

Preheat oven to 350°F (180°C).

Cook the carrots in boiling salted water until tender. Reserve ¹/₄ cup (60 mL) of the cooking liquid. Drain the carrots.

In a small bowl, combine the mayonnaise, reserved cooking liquid, onion, horseradish, salt, and pepper. Whisk well.

In a 9-inch (23 cm) square greased baking dish, arrange the carrots. Pour the sauce over top. Sprinkle with breadcrumbs, chopped parsley, and paprika. Dot with butter.

Bake uncovered for about 20 minutes. Serve hot.

Hunter Chicken

This is a delicious dish to serve on a cool autumn evening. It's comforting and homey. I learned this recipe while on a culinary trip to Italy. There, it's called Chicken Cacciatore.

SERVES 4 TO 6

1 **broiler chicken**, about 2 ¹/₂ lbs (1.1 kg), cut into breasts, thighs, and drumsticks, skin left on

2 tbsp (30 mL) **vegetable oil**

1 **onion**, peeled

2 cloves **garlic**, finely chopped

2 **carrots**, peeled and trimmed

1 cup (250 mL) **unoaked dry white wine**

2 cups (500 mL) **diced tomatoes**

1 cup (250 mL) **chicken stock**

1 sprig **rosemary**, stems removed and leaves finely chopped

salt and **pepper**, to taste

1 tbsp (15 mL) finely chopped **fresh parsley**

In a large skillet, brown the chicken pieces in the oil; season with salt and pepper. Remove the browned pieces to a plate. Drain off all but 1 tbsp (15 mL) of the pan drippings.

Meanwhile, in a food processor, finely chop the onion; add it and the chopped garlic to the hot skillet. Sauté for several minutes, scraping the browned bits off the bottom of the pan.

In the same food processor bowl, finely chop the carrots. Add them to the onion-garlic mixture and sauté for several minutes. Deglaze the pan with the white wine.

In the same food processor bowl, purée the tomatoes. Add them to the pan. along with the chicken stock and rosemary.

Return the partially cooked chicken pieces to the skillet and simmer uncovered for about 25 minutes, or until fully cooked.

Season with salt and pepper.

Garnish with finely chopped fresh parsley.

Chicken Stir-Fry with Broccoli and Carrots

This is a very healthy weeknight meal. Feel free to substitute cubes of tofu or slices of beef for the chicken.

SERVES 4

3/4 lb (340 g) **boneless, skinless chicken breasts**, thinly sliced

vegetable oil, for frying

1 tbsp (15 mL) minced **fresh ginger**

3 **carrots**, thinly sliced on the diagonal

half a head **broccoli**, sliced

1 **small onion**, cut into 1-inch (2.5 cm) wedges

1 **sweet pepper**, red, yellow or green, sliced into strips

2 **baby bok choy**, sliced

5 oz (140 g) **fresh spinach leaves**

3/4 cup (185 mL) **chicken broth**

1 tsp (5 mL) **cornstarch**

1/4 cup (60 mL) **oyster sauce**

1 tbsp (15 mL) **rice wine vinegar**

1 tsp (5 mL) **brown sugar**

2 to 3 tbsp (30 to 45 mL) **light soy sauce**

1 tbsp (15 mL) **Asian sesame oil**

2 tbsp (30 mL) **sesame seeds**

In a wok over high heat, add a small amount of oil and brown the chicken in batches, sprinkling with a little soy sauce. Remove each batch of browned chicken from the wok to a bowl and set aside.

Add a bit more oil to the wok and sauté the ginger, carrots, broccoli, and onion for several minutes. Add the pepper strips, bok choy, spinach leaves, and reserved browned chicken together with any chicken juices.

In a measuring cup, whisk together the chicken broth and cornstarch; whisk until no lumps remain. Pour over the vegetables. Add the oyster sauce, rice wine vinegar, brown sugar, and light soy sauce. Bring to a boil. Reduce the heat and cook several minutes until the sauce thickens.

Add the Asian sesame oil and the sesame seeds.

Serve over cooked white or brown rice.

Tarragon-Mustard Chicken

Here's a lovely dish that can be served as a weeknight meal or to dinner guests. Dijon mustard is featured here in a delicious creamy sauce.

SERVES 4

Unoaked Wine

The sauce in this recipe will reduce down during the cooking process. The reduction process intensifies all the flavours, even the oak in an oaked wine. Therefore, use an unoaked wine to avoid a bitter oak flavour in sauces.

4 boneless, skinless **chicken breasts**

1 tbsp (15 mL) **vegetable oil**

1 **shallot**, very finely chopped

$^1/_2$ cup (125 mL) **unoaked dry white wine**

$^1/_2$ cup (125 mL) **chicken stock**

$^1/_4$ cup (60 mL) **35% cream**

1 to 2 tsp (5 to 10 mL) **Dijon mustard**, or to taste

1 tsp (5 mL) **dried tarragon**

salt and **pepper**, to taste

chopped **fresh parsley**, for garnish

Between two sheets of waxed paper, use a rolling pin or a meat tenderizer mallet to pound each chicken breast to an even thickness, about $^3/_8$–inch (1 cm) thick. Season both sides of each breast with salt and pepper.

Over medium-high heat, brown the chicken breasts on both sides in the oil, then continue cooking until fully cooked, about 7 minutes. Remove the cooked breasts to a plate and keep warm.

Using the same pan, reduce the heat to medium and quickly sauté the shallot for about 30 seconds. Deglaze the pan with the wine. Let reduce slightly. Add the chicken stock and reduce the liquid by half. Add the cream, mustard, and tarragon. Let simmer until the sauce has thickened slightly. Season the sauce with salt and pepper.

Place the chicken on a platter and top with the sauce. Sprinkle with the chopped fresh parsley.

mustard
THE LITTLE SEED THAT CAN
....

Yellow mustard is the king of hot dog toppings. It's indispensible at family barbeques and sporting events, where children and adults alike top fat juicy wieners fitted into soft hotdog buns with thick wavy lines of the bright yellow stuff.

Nearly all of Canada's mustard production is grown by roughly 3,000 Saskatchewan farmers, making Saskatchewan the world's largest exporter of mustard seed. The unprocessed seed is exported in bulk to countries around the world, but particularly to the United States, Belgium, India, Japan, and Germany. Only one-third of mustard production remains in Canada to be milled into flour and condiments.

There are four types of mustard seed. Mild yellow seeds are milled to make dry mustard powder, mustard flour, and our beloved ballpark mustard. Spicy brown seeds are ground to make hotter mustards like the familiar French Dijon. The spicy oil from both the brown and the Oriental mustard seed is extracted and used in Asian cooking. Pungent black mustard seeds add kick to Indian cooking.

Brush prepared mustard on fish, pork, beef, or chicken destined for the smoker or grill, or use it as a delicious sticky base for breadings. A dollop of prepared mustard is a "must" in vinaigrettes and marinades. Mustard seeds are essential in Indian cooking. Nutritious mustard greens add a wonderful bite to a tossed salad or a stir-fry. If you are adventurous, try making your own mustard: each seed has its own personality.

Have fun! Experiment. You'll soon agree that mustard isn't just for the "dog." It adds wonderful character to nearly all your cooking.

SEEDS (TOP TO BOTTOM): yellow, brown, and black mustard seeds.

PASTES (TOP TO BOTTOM): Dijon, yellow ballpark, and old-style grainy.

Simple Broiled or Grilled Fish

Few dishes take less time to prepare than grilled or broiled fish. Here is one of my standard quick-and-easy weeknight meals. This recipe adapts easily whether you're cooking for one person or a group. The Dijon mustard is fabulous for bringing out flavour without leaving a strong mustardy taste to overwhelm the fish. Add a side salad and a crusty baguette, and you'll be eating in well under 30 minutes.

steelhead trout or salmon **steaks** or fillets, as required per person

vegetable oil or olive oil, for brushing

Dijon mustard, for brushing (regular, grainy, tarragon, or other flavour)

freshly cracked **black pepper**

Preheat broiler or barbeque.
Rinse the fish and pat dry with a paper towel.

TO BROIL STEAKS: Oil the broiling pan. Brush one side of each steak with oil, then slather on a good layer of Dijon mustard followed by cracked black pepper. Place the steak mustard side up on the pan and broil about 5 minutes. Turn the steaks and brush with oil, slather with mustard, and top with black pepper. Broil until done, about another 5 minutes, or until the fish just starts to flake.

TO BARBEQUE STEAKS: Oil the barbeque grates. Brush one side of each steak with oil, then slather on a good layer of Dijon mustard followed by cracked black pepper. Place the steak mustard side down on the grate and grill about 5 minutes. Brush the top of the steaks with oil, slather with mustard, and top with black pepper. Turn the steaks and grill until done, about another 5 minutes, or until the fish just starts to flake.

TO BROIL SKIN-ON FILLETS: Oil the broiling pan. Brush the flesh side of each fillet with oil, then slather on a good layer of Dijon mustard followed by cracked black pepper. Place the fillet mustard side up and skin side down on the pan and broil about 8 minutes, or until the fish just starts to flake.

TO BARBEQUE SKIN-ON FILLETS: Oil the barbeque grates. Brush the flesh side of each fillet with oil, then slather on a good layer of Dijon mustard followed by cracked black pepper. Place the fillet flesh side down and skin side up on the grates. Close the lid. Grill about 5 minutes. Turn over the fillets. Close the lid and grill another 3 to 5 minutes, or until the fish just starts to flake.

Fish Fritters with Easy Tartar Sauce

Here is a delicious and fun way to serve fish. The tartar sauce adds an old-fashioned, comforting element, reminiscent of the 1960s.

SERVES 4

1 lb (454 g) **firm boneless, skinless fish fillets**, such as pickerel, pike, perch, walleye, whitefish, or bass

1/2 cup (125 mL) **rice flour** or cornstarch

2 tbsp (30 mL) **unbleached all-purpose flour**

1 tsp (5 mL) **kosher salt**

1/2 tsp (2 mL) **cayenne powder**

1/2 tsp (2 mL) **onion powder**

1/4 tsp (1 mL) ground **black pepper**

1/2 tsp (2 mL) **chili powder**

1 **egg**, beaten

1/2 cup (125 mL) **cold water**

1/2 cup (125 mL) **corn kernels**, frozen

3 **green onions**, finely sliced

vegetable oil, for deep frying

sea salt, for sprinkling

Jeff Matity, fishing biologist and outdoor educator, shows off a Northern pike caught at Last Mountain Lake, SK.

Rinse the fish and pat dry with a paper towel. Roughly chop the fish fillets with a knife into 1/2-inch (1.5 cm) chunks.

To make the batter, in a medium bowl, combine the rice flour, unbleached all-purpose flour, salt, cayenne powder, onion powder, ground black pepper, and chili powder. Whisk in the egg and cold water to create a smooth batter. Add the chopped fish along with the corn kernels and green onions. Stir to coat well.

In a deep medium-sized pot, heat no more than 1 inch (2.5 cm) vegetable oil to 350°F (180°C). Drop spoonfuls of the fish batter into the hot oil and cook for about 3 to 5 minutes, or until golden brown and cooked through. With a slotted spoon, remove the cooked fritters to a paper towel to drain and cool slightly. Sprinkle lightly with sea salt. Serve warm with the Easy Tartar Sauce.

Easy Tartar Sauce

1/2 cup (125 mL) **mayonnaise**

1/2 tsp (2 mL) **Dijon mustard**

1 to 2 tbsp (15 to 30 mL) **green hot dog relish**

In a small bowl, whisk together the mayonnaise, Dijon mustard, and hot dog relish. Taste and adjust ingredients. Chill until ready to serve.

Beef Curry with Scented Rice

Add some exotic flavour to your weekday cooking. Fenugreek and garam masala (a ground mixture of Indian spices) can be found in the herb and spice section of your supermarket, or at a specialty food store. This recipe is best made one day ahead to allow the flavours to develop.

SERVES 4 TO 6

2 **onions**

3 cloves **garlic**, peeled

1 lb (454 g) **ground beef** or bison

2 tsp (10 mL) minced **fresh ginger**

1 ½ tbsp (22 mL) **Indian-style curry paste**, such as Patak's Madras-style

2 tsp (10 mL) **garam masala**

1 tsp (5 mL) **ground turmeric**

1 can (14 oz/398 mL) **diced tomatoes**

1 ½ cups (375 mL) **beef stock**

1 tbsp (15 mL) **fenugreek leaves**, optional

1 tsp (5 mL) **kosher salt**

1 **apple**, grated

¾ cup (185 mL) **coconut milk**

vegetable oil, for sautéing

In a food processor, finely chop the onion and garlic together.

Sauté the ground meat in a large pot over medium-high heat until browned. Drain off any fat and remove the cooked meat to a separate bowl. In the same pot as you browned the meat, add 1 tbsp (15 mL) vegetable oil and the onion-garlic mixture and sauté for several minutes. Do not brown. Add the ginger, curry paste, garam masala, and turmeric. Sauté, stirring constantly, for at least one minute to toast the spices.

Return the browned meat to the pot and add the tomatoes, beef stock, fenugreek leaves, salt, and apple. Bring to a boil, reduce the heat, and let simmer 30 to 60 minutes, until all the liquid has evaporated and the mixture is quite thick.

Add the coconut milk and warm through. Do not boil.

Serve over the Scented Rice.

Scented Rice

2 cups (500 mL) **basmati rice**

3 ½ cups (875 mL) **water**

1 **cinnamon stick**

1 tsp (5 mL) **ground turmeric**

1 **black cardamom pod**, bruised to expose seeds

½ tsp (2 mL) **kosher salt**

2 tbsp (30 mL) **vegetable oil** or olive oil

Rinse the basmati rice with cold water. In a medium pot, bring the water to a boil. Add the rinsed basmati rice, cinnamon stick, turmeric, black cardamom pod, salt, and oil. Stir, reduce to low heat, and cover with a lid. Simmer until the rice is tender and the water has been absorbed, about 20 minutes. Remove the cinnamon stick and cardamom pod and fluff the rice with a fork. Cover and let stand another 5 to 10 minutes before serving.

Simmental Hereford cross, Stoney Beach, SK.

Blackened Steaks with Creamy Mushroom Sauce

Our family often enjoys this meal on a Friday night at the end of a long week. A tossed salad, a great baguette, and a glass of wine is all I need to add for a quick meal that satisfies everyone around the table.

SERVES 4

4 **bison** or beef **steaks**, rib-eyes or strip loins, cut 1 1/4-inch (3 cm) thick

vegetable oil, for drizzling

steak spice, such as JB's Blackened Saskatchewan Steak Spice or Montreal Steak Spice, or salt and a generous amount of cracked black pepper

2 tbsp (30 mL) **unsalted butter**

3/4 lb (340 g) **mushrooms** such as button, cremini, chanterelles, shiitake, morels, or a mixture of several varieties

salt and **pepper**, to taste

2 tsp (10 mL) **fresh thyme leaves**, or 1 tsp (5 mL) dried thyme

1/2 cup (125 mL), or more, **35% cream**

Fresh morels.

Heat a sauté pan on medium-high heat.

Oil both sides of the steaks with a small amount of oil, and sprinkle both sides with the steak seasoning, or with salt and a generous amount of cracked black pepper. Place steaks in the hot sauté pan and cook about 5 to 7 minutes per side for rare to medium rare, or until desired doneness.

Remove to a plate. Drape with a sheet of waxed paper and cover with a tea towel. Let rest 10 minutes.

Meanwhile in the same sauté pan, add the butter and mushrooms; season with salt and pepper. Cook, stirring occasionally, until all the liquid from the mushrooms has evaporated. Add thyme leaves and cream, and let simmer until slightly thickened, about 10 minutes. Taste and adjust seasonings.

Place the steaks on individual dinner plates. Pour any drippings back into the sauce and let simmer another minute or so before serving.

Serve the steaks with the mushroom sauce.

bison
THE SPIRIT OF THE WEST

From the time of the ice age, large herds of migratory bison have roamed the prairies. The large ruminant was the lord of the plains, able to adapt to a warming climate unlike the now-extinct saber-toothed tiger and woolly mammoth.

The bison was highly valued by North American indigenous peoples, who regarded it as a special gift from the Creator. Indeed, the bison was crucial to their survival. Its flesh supplied a concentrated source of protein, the hide provided clothing and shelter, the fat gave fuel, and bones were fashioned into tools.

At one time, between 30 million and 60 million of these gigantic creatures roamed the North American prairie. Sadly, by 1900, just 1,000 of these majestic animals remained; greed and uncontrolled hunting had decimated the population to near-extinction. Concerted efforts by ranchers and conservationists have revived the population, which now numbers over 400,000 in North America. About 200,000 are in Canada, mostly concentrated in Western Canada, with roughly 49% grazing naturally in Alberta, 29% in Saskatchewan, and 10% in Manitoba. North America is the only major supplier of bison to the world.

Demand for bison is growing, as consumers increasingly want to know where their food comes from, how it's produced, and what environmental impacts animals have on the environment. Health-conscious consumers are attracted to bison meat for its flavour, leanness, and high concentrations of iron, zinc, protein, and essential fatty acids. Internationally, Europeans, particularly the French and the Germans, enjoy the taste of bison. It's a natural product associated with Canada's pristine environment and its indigenous peoples.

Today's bison are trimmer and smaller than their heritage counterparts. Because it is not bred for marbling, the meat is quite lean and can't be cooked in the same manner as beef. Roasts and steaks are best roasted or grilled to medium or medium rare because these cuts become tough when overcooked. Ground bison is fabulous when made into a burger, and should be grilled to the point where the pink has just barely disappeared. Bison ribs and stewing meats are fantastic when braised long and slow.

Try bison. It is a fabulous choice if you're looking for a tasty and healthy protein, and a deep and historical connection to the food on your plate.

FACING PAGE, BOTTOM LEFT: Rancher Bernie Kot inspects the herd.

FACING PAGE AND ABOVE: Bison at K-1 Bison Ranch, Weyburn, SK.

123

Bison and Broccoli Stir-Fry

A super-quick and healthy family meal. Feel free to substitute beef for the bison.

SERVES 4

1 lb (454 g) **bison round steak**, trimmed and frozen for 1 hour

1 tbsp (15 mL) **vegetable oil**

3 cloves **garlic**, chopped

1-inch (2.5 cm) piece **fresh ginger**, peeled and chopped

1 **onion**, sliced into thin wedges

2 cups (500 mL) **broccoli florets**

1 **carrot**, peeled and cut on the diagonal into slices

1 **red pepper**, cut into strips

2 tbsp (30 mL) **soy sauce**

1 tsp (5 mL) **brown sugar**

$^1/_2$ tsp (2 mL) **chili flakes**, or more

2 tbsp (30 mL) **rice wine vinegar**

2 tbsp (30 mL) **hoisin sauce**

1 $^1/_2$ cups (375 mL) **beef broth**

1 tbsp (15 mL) **cornstarch**

1 tbsp (15 mL) **Asian sesame oil**

1 cup (250 mL) **fresh bean sprouts**

cilantro leaves, for garnish

Slice the partially frozen meat on the diagonal into very thin strips.

Heat the oil in a wok over high heat. Sauté the garlic and ginger for about 30 seconds. Add the sliced bison, and brown in two or three batches, being careful not to crowd the pan. As each batch is browned, remove it to a bowl.

Add onion, broccoli florets, carrot, and red pepper to the wok. Stir to combine. Let cook several minutes.

Return the browned meat to the wok along with the soy sauce, brown sugar, chili flakes, rice wine vinegar, and hoisin sauce.

Stir together the beef broth and cornstarch, and pour about 1 cup (250 mL) over the stir-fry. Bring to a boil to thicken sauce. If you prefer a "saucier" stir-fry, add more of the broth-cornstarch mixture. Drizzle with Asian sesame oil.

Serve over white or brown rice. Top each serving with fresh bean sprouts and several cilantro leaves.

Without a Doubt, The Best Spaghetti Sauce

Shortly before I went to university, I lived with my father in the small town of Berwyn, Alberta. The old sign at the entrance to the town read: "Population 50 and Growing." While there, I worked as a cashier at a supermarket in nearby Grimshaw. An Italian man frequently came in to purchase ingredients for his spaghetti sauce. Try as I might, I never could weasel the recipe from him, but he did tell me that he always put in carrots and red wine. Here's my version, which I've been making and perfecting ever since.

SERVES 6 TO 8

2 **medium onions**, chopped

4 cloves **garlic**, finely chopped

2 stalks **celery**, diced into ¼-inch (5 mm) cubes

1 medium **carrot**, diced into ¼-inch (5 mm) cubes

2 tbsp (30 mL) **vegetable oil**

2 lbs (907 g) **ground beef** or bison

1 can (28 oz/796 mL) **diced tomatoes**

1 can (7 ½ oz/227 mL) **tomato sauce**, such as Hunt's (not spaghetti sauce)

1 can (10 oz/284 mL) **condensed tomato soup**, such as Campbell's

1 cup (250 mL) **Italian red wine**

10 oz (284 mL) **beef broth**

2 **bay leaves**

3 tbsp (45 mL) **Worcestershire sauce**

½ tsp (2 mL) **chili flakes**, or more

1 tsp (5 mL) **black pepper**

2 tsp (10 mL) **dried oregano**, preferably Greek oregano

1 tsp (5 mL) **dried basil leaves**

1 tsp (5 mL) **salt**

¾ lb (340 g) **raw button** or cremini **mushrooms**, thinly sliced

In a large Dutch oven or deep pot over medium heat, sauté the onion, garlic, celery, and carrots in the oil until they are translucent, about 5 minutes. Transfer the vegetables to a bowl.

Without adding more oil to the pot, brown the meat until all traces of red have disappeared. With a bulb baster, siphon off all the juice and fat into a glass measuring cup. There will be virtually no juices if you are using bison.

Add the reserved cooked vegetables to the meat in the pot. Add the tomatoes, tomato sauce, tomato soup, red wine, beef broth, bay leaves, Worcestershire sauce, chili flakes, black pepper, oregano, basil, and salt.

Using a bulb baster, siphon off the drippings that have settled to the bottom of the glass measuring cup, leaving the fat that has risen to the top. Add the drippings back to the meat mixture, together with enough water to measure 1 cup (250 ml).

Add the mushrooms. Bring the mixture to a boil and simmer over low heat for 3 hours. Stir often, about every 20 minutes. When the mixture is thick and the liquid has evaporated, taste and adjust seasonings, adding more herbs or salt, as needed.

Serve over al dente cooked noodles (spaghetti, spaghettini, or capellini). Top with freshly grated Parmesan cheese.

Chili Con Carne

There are two secrets to a great chili: fresh pungent spices and dark chocolate. Both add a deep layer of flavour to the chili. I've also added chipotle pepper to give this dish a wonderful smoky note.

SERVES 6 TO 8

2 lbs (907 g) **ground bison** or beef

1 **large onion**, chopped

4 cloves **garlic**, peeled and finely chopped

1 tbsp (15 mL) **vegetable oil**

2 tbsp (30 mL) **chili powder**, or more

1 tsp (5 mL) **ground cumin**

1 can (28 oz/796 mL) **diced plum tomatoes**

1 can (5 ^{1}/$_2$ oz/170 mL) **tomato paste**

20 oz (568 mL) **beef broth**

^{3}/$_4$ cup (185 mL) **salsa**, mild, medium, or hot

1 tbsp (15 mL) finely chopped **chipotle pepper** or smoked paprika

^{1}/$_4$ tsp (1 mL) **thyme leaves**

1 oz (28 g) **70% dark chocolate**, chopped

1 tsp (5 mL) freshly ground **black pepper**

^{1}/$_2$ tsp (2 mL), or more, **chili flakes** (optional)

1 ^{1}/$_2$ cups (375 mL) **corn niblets**, fresh or frozen

1 can (28 oz/796 mL) **red kidney beans**, drained and rinsed well

1 tsp (5 mL) **kosher salt**

grated **Monterey Jack cheese**, for topping

tortilla chips or fresh buns

In a Dutch oven or large deep pot, brown the ground meat on medium-high heat until no traces of red remain. Siphon off any drippings into a glass measuring cup. There will be virtually no juices if you are using bison. Set aside for later use. Transfer browned meat to a bowl.

Sauté the onion and garlic in the oil over medium heat until they are translucent. Add the chili powder and cumin and stir constantly for one minute to toast the spices.

Return the browned meat to the pot and add the tomatoes, tomato paste, broth, salsa, chipotle pepper or smoked paprika, thyme leaves, chocolate, black pepper, and chili flakes. Using a bulb baster, siphon any drippings from glass measuring cup, leaving the fat that has risen to the top. Add the drippings to the meat-tomato mixture. Stir.

Simmer over low heat, uncovered, for 1 ^{1}/$_2$ to 2 hours. Stir often, about every 20 minutes. Add the corn and kidney beans and continue to simmer until the chili is thick, another 60 minutes. Add salt. Taste and adjust seasonings.

Spoon the chili into bowls and top with grated Monterey Jack cheese. Serve with tortilla chips or fresh buns.

Pale Ale Braised Pork Belly

Leo Pantel was one of the first chefs I met upon moving to Regina. He's passionate about serving local products, and has done so for dignitaries, entertainers, and the Queen of England. Over the years he's become a close personal friend and I'm delighted to share his recipe for pork belly, an "old school" pork cut popular with chefs throughout the province. This is one of those "set it and forget it" recipes. Store any extra cure for the next time you make this recipe. You can also use this recipe with beef short ribs, in which case, change the chicken stock to beef stock.

SERVES 4 TO 6

Chef Leo Pantel.

1 **pork belly piece**, about 2 lbs (907 g), preferably skin on, approximately 2 inches (5 cm) wide and 4 to 5 inches (10 to 12 cm) long

$^1/_2$ cup (125 mL) or more, **Leo's Pork Dry Cure** (recipe on facing page)

1 $^1/_2$ tbsp (22 mL) **vegetable oil**

3 cups (750 mL) *mirepoix* (a combination of diced onion, celery and carrot)

1 **bay leaf**

3 to 4 sprigs **fresh thyme**

2 $^2/_3$ cups (660 mL) **pale ale beer**

6 cups (1.5 L) **chicken stock**

salt and freshly ground **black pepper**, to taste

Rinse the pork and dry with paper towels. Season the meat well on all sides with the cure and pack it into a plastic container; seal. Refrigerate and allow the pork to cure for two days. After curing, rinse the pork under cold water to remove all the seasoning. Pat dry.

Preheat oven to 350°F (180°C).

Heat a heavy, medium-sized ovenproof Dutch oven or large stockpot over medium-high heat. Season the pork belly with salt and pepper. Add the oil to the pot and sear the pork on each side to a deep, golden brown. Remove the pork to a plate and pour out any excess fat, leaving about 1 tbsp (15 mL) in the pot.

Add the mirepoix to the pot and cook until the vegetables begin to soften and are slightly caramelized; stir occasionally. If the mixture begins to burn, add a very small amount of water to the pot and scrape any brown bits off the bottom. Add the bay leaf, thyme, and beer. Bring to a simmer and reduce by half.

Return the pork to the pot and add the chicken stock. Bring to a simmer; skim off any visible scum and fat. Cover with a tight-fitting lid and place the pot into the oven on the center rack. Cook until fork tender, about 3 hours.

Transfer the meat to a platter; cover and keep warm. Strain out the mirepoix and the herbs; reserve the liquid. Discard vegetables and herbs. Transfer the liquid back to the pot, skim off any fat, and bring to a simmer. Reduce the liquid by two-thirds, until about 2 cups (500 mL) remain. Taste and adjust seasonings.

Cut the meat into individual serving pieces, and place on top of mashed potatoes or smashed fingerling potatoes. Top with some sauce.

Leo's Pork Dry Cure
MAKES ABOUT 1 CUP (250 ML)

3 tbsp (45 mL) **whole black peppercorns**

2 tbsp (30 mL) **whole cloves**

5 tbsp (75 mL) **dark brown sugar**

2 **cinnamon sticks**, ground and blended in spice mill, or about 1 tbsp (15 mL) ground cinnamon

3 tbsp (45 mL) **coarse sea salt**

Mix the whole black peppercorns, whole cloves, dark brown sugar, ground cinnamon sticks, and coarse sea salt together.

Apple Cake with Lemon Sauce

As a young teenager, I was already well into baking and loved experimenting. One day, I imagined, then created, this delicious autumn cake. It has since become a favourite recipe, and one that my brother Ethan used in his younger days to impress his girlfriends.

MAKES ONE 8-INCH (20 CM) SQUARE CAKE

4 cups (1 L) thinly sliced, peeled and cored **apples**, such as Gala or Spartan

1 tbsp (15 mL) **lemon juice**

¹/₂ cup (125 mL) **granulated sugar**

¹/₄ cup (60 mL) **water**

1 ¹/₃ cup (330 mL) **unbleached all-purpose flour**

³/₄ cup (185 mL) **granulated sugar**

3 tsp (15 mL) **baking powder**

¹/₂ tsp (2 mL) **kosher salt**

¹/₄ cup (60 mL) frozen **shortening**

1 **egg**, beaten lightly with a fork

³/₄ cup (185 mL) **milk**

Preheat oven to 350°F (180°C).

Grease the cake pan. Lay the sliced apples in the bottom of the pan.

In a small bowl or glass measuring cup, mix the lemon juice, ¹/₂ cup (125 mL) granulated sugar, and water to form a syrup. Pour the syrup over the apples.

Scoop the flour gently into measuring cups. Level the top with the flat edge of a knife and transfer the flour to a medium bowl. Add ³/₄ cup (185 mL) granulated sugar, baking powder, and salt.

Using a box grater, grate in the frozen shortening, sweeping up some of the flour as you grate the fat. The shortening-flour mixture should resemble coarse cornmeal. Make a hollow in the centre of the flour mixture and add the egg and milk. Gently mix with a spatula until the dry ingredients are just moist. Do not overmix. Spread the batter on top of the apples.

Bake for about 45 minutes, or until a toothpick inserted into the centre comes out clean. Serve warm with the Lemon Sauce.

Lemon Sauce

¹/₂ cup (125 mL) **granulated sugar**

1 tbsp (15 mL) **cornstarch**

¹/₄ cup (60 mL) **cold water**

¹/₂ cup (125 mL) **boiling water**

2 tbsp (30 mL) **unsalted butter**

2 tbsp (30 mL) **fresh lemon juice**

In a saucepan, mix together the granulated sugar and cornstarch. Whisk in the cold water. Add the boiling water. Cook over medium heat, whisking constantly until thickened. Add the unsalted butter and stir until melted. Add the fresh lemon juice and set aside to cool.

Apple Cake with Caramel Glaze

Apples and caramel—they're the perfect combination. Use the extra Cinnamon Spice Mix as an apple or pumpkin pie spice, or for hot cross buns.

MAKES ONE BUNDT CAKE

2 cups (500 mL) **unbleached all-purpose flour**

1 tsp (5 mL) **baking soda**

1 tsp (5 mL) **kosher salt**

2 tsp (10 mL) **Cinnamon Spice Mix**

3 **eggs**

2 tsp (10 mL) **pure vanilla extract**

1 cup (250 mL) **granulated sugar**

1 cup (250 mL) **vegetable oil**

3 cups (750 mL) finely sliced, peeled, and cored **apples**

¾ cup (185 mL) **raisins**

CARAMEL GLAZE

½ cup (125 mL) **brown sugar**

¼ cup (60 mL) **salted butter**

1 tsp (5 mL) **vanilla**

¼ cup (60 mL) **heavy 35% cream**

Preheat oven to 350°F (180°C). Butter and flour a standard Bundt or tube pan.

Scoop the flour gently into the measuring cups. Level the top with the flat edge of a knife and transfer the flour to a medium bowl. Add the baking soda, salt, and 2 tsp (10 mL) of the Cinnamon Spice Mix. Whisk to combine and set aside.

In a large bowl, whisk the eggs by hand for about 1 minute. Whisk in the vanilla extract. Whisk in the sugar gradually, followed by the vegetable oil in a slow steady stream. Add the flour mixture all at once and stir with a spatula until just moistened. Fold in the apples and raisins.

Transfer the batter to the prepared pan and bake for about 50 minutes. Let cool 10 minutes before removing the cake to a wire rack to cool. Cool completely.

CARAMEL GLAZE: Melt the brown sugar and butter in a saucepan. Add the vanilla and cream. Bring to a boil and simmer 1 to 2 minutes. Let cool to the consistency of molasses before drizzling on the cake.

Cinnamon Spice Mix
MAKES ABOUT ⅓ CUP (80 ML)

6 tsp (30 mL) **ground cinnamon**

2½ tsp (12 mL) **ground ginger**

3 tsp (15 mL) **ground coriander**

1 tsp (5 mL) *each* **ground nutmeg** and **ground allspice**

Combine the cinnamon, ginger, coriander, nutmeg, and allspice in a bowl. Store the extra mix at room temperature in a jar.

Pumpkin Raisin Cake

This superb cake is delicious and stays very moist.

MAKES ONE BUNDT CAKE

2 1/2 cups (625 mL) **unbleached all-purpose flour**

1 cup (250 mL) **stone-ground, whole wheat flour**

1 tsp (5 mL) **baking powder**

1 tsp (5 mL) **baking soda**

1 tsp (5 mL) **ground cinnamon**

1 tsp (5 mL) **kosher salt**

1/2 tsp (2 mL) **ground cloves**

1/2 tsp (2 mL) **ground nutmeg**

1 cup (250 mL) **granulated sugar**

1 cup (250 mL) **brown sugar**

2/3 cup (160 mL) **unsalted butter**, room temperature

4 **eggs**

2 cups (500 mL) **cooked pure pumpkin** (do not use pumpkin pie filling)

2/3 cup (160 mL) **dark rum** (water or milk can be substituted)

1 cup (250 mL) **raisins**

Preheat oven to 350°F (180°C). Butter and flour a standard Bundt or tube pan.

Scoop the unbleached all-purpose and whole wheat flour gently into the measuring cups. Level the top with the flat edge of a knife and transfer the flour to a medium bowl. Add the baking powder, baking soda, cinnamon, salt, cloves, and nutmeg. Stir and set aside.

In a large bowl, beat the granulated sugar, brown sugar, and butter together until light. Beat in the eggs, one at a time, until well mixed. Add the pumpkin purée, and then the dark rum.

In two additions, add the dry ingredients, until just mixed together. Stir in the raisins.

Transfer the batter to the prepared pan. Bake for 70 minutes, or until a toothpick inserted into the cake comes out clean.

Remove from oven and let rest 10 minutes before removing cake from the pan to a wire rack to cool.

When cool, place the cake on a decorative plate and drizzle the cake with the Icing Sugar Glaze.

Icing Sugar Glaze

1 cup (250 mL) **icing sugar**

1 to 2 tbsp (15 to 30 mL) **milk**

1/4 tsp (1 mL) **pure almond** or vanilla **extract**

In a small bowl, whisk together the icing sugar, milk, and almond or vanilla extract to make a smooth icing.

Freshly picked mini pumpkins at Lincoln Gardens, Lumsden, SK.

Apple Wontons

These decadent little turnovers are a delight. To me, they are reminiscent of the Sunshine Beavertails that are popular outdoor treats in Canada's capital.

MAKES ABOUT 12

---

¹/₄ cup (60 mL) **unsalted butter**

2 **Granny Smith apples**, peeled, cored, and chopped into ¹/₂-inch (1.5 cm) cubes

2 tbsp (30 mL) packed **brown sugar**

pinch **kosher salt**

1 tbsp (15 mL) **dark rum**

about 12 **wonton** or egg roll **wrappers***

1 **egg**, beaten

vegetable oil, for frying

Cinnamon Sugar, for sprinkling

1 **lemon**, cut into wedges

Melt the butter in a medium skillet over medium heat. Add the cubed apples and sauté until tender, about 5 minutes. Add the brown sugar and season with salt. Stir to dissolve sugar. Very carefully add the rum (it will bubble and spatter). Stir until a slightly thick sauce forms. Set aside to cool to room temperature.

Heat a clean medium or large skillet over medium heat. Add about 1 inch (2.5 cm) oil for shallow frying and heat to 365°F (185°C).

To prepare the wrappers, lay one wonton sheet on a clean counter. Brush along the edges with a bit of beaten egg. Spoon about 1 tbsp (15 mL) apple mixture onto the centre of the wrapper. Fold over to create a triangular turnover. Press edges to seal. Repeat the procedure with the remaining wontons.

Add 2 to 3 wontons to the hot oil. Working quickly, turn them over immediately and let them cook for about 5 to 10 seconds. Turn over and brown the other side. Remove to a plate and immediately sprinkle with the Cinnamon Sugar and squeeze over fresh lemon juice. Serve warm, on their own or with vanilla ice cream.

*Wonton and egg roll wrappers are available in the produce section of most larger supermarkets, and at Asian specialty stores.

Apples from Over the Hill Orchards, Lumsden, SK.

Cinnamon Sugar

---

3 tbsp (45 mL) **granulated sugar**

1 tsp (5 mL) **ground cinnamon**

Combine the sugar and ground cinnamon in a small bowl.

Apple Dumplings

Here's an old-fashioned dessert that needs a good revival. I can't prepare this homey dish without thinking of my maternal grandmother, who made these every autumn. I remember her sprinkling the brown sugar and spices over the dumplings, never measuring a thing. Aren't grandmothers like that? She poured milk into the bottom of the pan and the dumplings came out crispy on top and slightly soft on the bottom. She always served them warm in a bowl with more milk.

SERVES 6

1 recipe **Basic Flaky Pastry** (recipe on page 86)

6 medium **apples**, peeled and cored (Prairie Sun, Gala, and Spartan apples work well)

brown sugar

raisins

ground cinnamon

freshly grated nutmeg

about ¹/₃ cup (80 mL) **soft butter**

6 **whole cloves**

1 **egg**, beaten

about 1 cup (250 mL) **milk**

additional **brown sugar**

additional **soft butter**

Preheat oven to 425°F (220°C).

Prepare pastry dough as directed on page 86. Refrigerate the two balls of dough while you peel and core the apples.

Roll out one ball of dough to an 18- × 6-inch (46 × 15 cm) rectangle. Using a knife or pizza wheel, cut the dough into three 6-inch (15 cm) squares. Place one apple on each square. Fill the empty core half full with brown sugar. Add some raisins and fill with additional brown sugar. Top with a few more raisins. Sprinkle the stuffed apple liberally with ground cinnamon and nutmeg. Top each apple with 1 tsp (5 mL) soft butter.

Brush the corners of each square with a bit of beaten egg. Bring the opposite corners of the dough up to the top of the apple to create a four-cornered package. Seal.

Repeat the procedure with the second ball of dough.

Reroll the pastry scraps and cut out three leaves for the top of each dumpling. Use beaten egg to "glue" them to the pastry. Insert a whole clove into the top of each apple to create a stem. Brush the dumplings with beaten egg, and set inside a greased baking dish large enough to hold the six dumplings.

Pour about 1 cup (250 mL) milk into the dish around the base of the dumplings to come ¹/₄-inch (5 mm) up the sides of the dish. Sprinkle the milk with a small handful of brown sugar. Be careful not to sprinkle the sugar onto the dumplings because the sugar will burn. Drop 3 to 4 tsp (15 to 20 mL) soft butter into the milk.

Bake for 15 minutes. Reduce heat to 350°F (180°C) and bake for another 35 minutes. Serve warm, on their own, in a bowl with additional milk, or with vanilla ice cream.

Old-Fashioned Apple Pie

Many varieties of apples grow on the prairies. Prairie Sun is one of the most popular for making pies as it has a fairly long shelf life, over six months in your crisper. It is also a popular eating apple. Enjoy this apple pie with a scoop of vanilla ice cream.

MAKES ONE 9-INCH (23 CM) DOUBLE-CRUST PIE

1 recipe **Basic Flaky Pastry** (recipe on page 86)

6 medium **apples**, such as Prairie Sun, Gala, Spartan, or Granny Smith

$1/2$ cup (125 mL) packed **brown sugar**

1 tsp (5 mL) **ground cinnamon**

$1/2$ tsp (2 mL) freshly grated **nutmeg**

$1 1/2$ tbsp (22 mL) **soft butter**

1 **egg**, beaten

1 tbsp (15 mL) **granulated sugar**, for sprinkling

Preheat oven to 425°F (220°C).

Prepare the pastry dough as directed for the unbaked double crust pie, on page 86. Chill for 30 minutes while preparing the filling.

Peel, core, and thinly slice the apples.

In a large bowl, combine the sliced apples, brown sugar, cinnamon, and nutmeg.

Remove the chilled pie crust from the refrigerator. Remove the folded top crust from the pie plate. Transfer the prepared apple mixture to the bottom pie crust. Dot with bits of the butter. Top with the second pie crust. Seal and trim the edges, and make slits in the top crust for steam to escape.

Brush the crust with beaten egg, and sprinkle it with about 1 tbsp (15 mL) granulated sugar.

Bake for 15 minutes. Reduce the heat to 350°F (180°C) and bake for another 35 minutes.

Serve warm or at room temperature.

Pumpkin Pie

This pumpkin pie is the one I enjoyed every Thanksgiving as I was growing up. The recipe strikes a delicious balance between pumpkin and spices. It's the best pumpkin pie I've ever tasted.

MAKES ONE 9-INCH (23 CM) PIE

$^1/_2$ recipe **Basic Flaky Pastry**
(recipe on page 86)

2 **eggs**

$^3/_4$ cup (185 mL) **evaporated milk**

$^1/_2$ cup (125 mL) **milk**

1 cup (250 mL) **canned pure pumpkin**
(Do not use pumpkin pie filling.)

$^1/_2$ tbsp (7 mL) **cornstarch**

$^1/_3$ cup (80 mL) packed **brown sugar**

2 tbsp (30 mL) **granulated sugar**

$^1/_2$ tsp (2 mL) **ground cinnamon**

$^1/_8$ tsp (.5 mL) **ground allspice**

$^1/_8$ tsp (.5 mL) **powdered ginger**

$^1/_4$ tsp (1 mL) **kosher salt**

ground nutmeg, for sprinkling

Prepare the single-crust pastry dough recipe as directed on page 86. Line a 9-inch (23 cm) pie plate with the crust. Trim and flute the edges of the crust. Refrigerate for at least 30 minutes.

Prick the cold unbaked crust all over with a fork. Bake the crust at 425°F (220°C) for 20 minutes. Remove from the oven and cool on a wire rack.

Reduce oven temperature to 350°F (180°C).

Whisk the eggs, evaporated milk, milk, and pumpkin together in a bowl. Add the cornstarch, brown sugar, granulated sugar, cinnamon, allspice, ginger, and salt. Whisk well to make sure there are no lumps.

Pour the filling into the partially baked pie crust. Sprinkle the top lightly with nutmeg. Very carefully transfer the pie to the hot oven.

Bake 30 to 40 minutes, until a knife inserted into the centre of the pie comes out clean. Let the pie cool completely. Refrigerate until ready to serve.

Cut into wedges and serve with lightly sweetened whipped cream.

Pumpkins at Corn Maiden Market, Lumsden, SK.

Pumpkin Muffins

Here's a delicious way to use up leftover pumpkin. This recipe is also delicious made into a loaf and enjoyed with a cup of tea.

MAKES 16 LARGE MUFFINS

1 cup (250 mL) **unbleached all-purpose flour**

1 cup (250 mL) **stone-ground, whole wheat flour**

1/2 cup (125 mL) **granulated sugar**

2 tsp (10 mL) **baking powder**

1 tsp (5 mL) **baking soda**

1 tsp (5 mL) **ground cinnamon**

1/2 tsp (2 mL) **kosher salt**

1/4 tsp (1 mL) **ground ginger**

1/3 cup (80 mL) **plain yogurt**

1 1/2 cups (375 mL) **milk**

1/4 cup (60 mL) **vegetable oil**

1 **egg**

3/4 cup (185 mL) **puréed unsweetened pure pumpkin** (Do not use pumpkin pie filling.)

3/4 cup (185 mL) **chopped nuts**, such as walnuts or pecans

Preheat oven to 400°F (200°C). Grease 16 muffin cups or line them with paper muffin cups.

Combine the unbleached all-purpose flour, whole wheat flour, sugar, baking powder, baking soda, cinnamon, salt, and ginger in a medium bowl. Stir to combine.

In another bowl, whisk together the yogurt, milk, oil, egg, and pumpkin. Mix well. Add to the dry ingredients and mix until almost combined. Add the nuts and continue to mix until combined. Do not overmix. Transfer batter to muffins cups.

Bake for 18 to 20 minutes.

Remove from the oven, and let stand 10 minutes before removing from the pans to wire racks to cool completely.

LOAF VARIATION: Preheat oven to 325°F (165°C). Grease a 9- × 5-inch (2 L) loaf pan and line the bottom with parchment paper. Prepare the batter as for the muffins and transfer to loaf pan. Bake for 70 to 90 minutes. Remove from the oven, and let stand 10 minutes before removing from the pan to a wire rack to cool completely.

Wholesome Pancakes

At our house, my sons mutiny if I don't make pancakes or waffles on Sundays. To ensure that I'm still giving my family a wholesome meal, I've created some power-packed recipes that turn a sweet empty-calorie breakfast into something quite nutritious. These pancakes are still as fluffy as you'd expect them to be because of the addition of buttermilk and the folding in of beaten egg whites.

SERVES 4 TO 6

³/₄ cup (185 mL) **unbleached all-purpose flour**

¹/₂ cup (125 mL) **stone-ground, whole wheat flour**

¹/₄ cup (60 mL) **ground flax**

¹/₄ cup (60 mL) finely chopped **toasted almonds**

1 tsp (5 mL) **baking powder**

1 tsp (5 mL) **baking soda**

¹/₂ tsp (2 mL) **ground cinnamon**

¹/₂ tsp (2 mL) **kosher salt**

3 tbsp (45 mL) **granulated sugar**

1 ripe **banana**, mashed

about ³/₄ cup (185 mL) **buttermilk**

1 small **apple**, peeled, cored and finely chopped

3 **eggs**, separated

3 tbsp (45 mL) **unsalted butter**, melted

In a large mixing bowl, combine the unbleached all-purpose flour, whole wheat flour, flax, almonds, baking power, baking soda, cinnamon, salt, and sugar. Mix well. Set aside.

In a small bowl, mash the banana until smooth. Transfer the mashed banana to a glass measuring cup. Add enough buttermilk to make 1 ¹/₂ cups (375 ml).

Combine the banana-buttermilk mixture with the apple, egg yolks and melted butter. Mix well. Stir the banana-buttermilk mixture into the flour mixture until just combined.

In a clean bowl, free of any traces of grease, beat the egg whites until stiff but not dry. Stir one quarter of the beaten egg whites into the batter to lighten. Gently fold the remainder of the beaten egg whites into the batter until no traces of white remain.

Heat a large skillet over medium heat. Add a small amount of butter. Add the batter to the hot skillet in heaping spoonfuls. Cook until bubbles break through the surface and the sides are slightly set. Turn the pancakes and cook the second side another minute or so. To test for doneness, gently press the centre of each pancake with your finger. If it springs back, it's done.

Serve with maple syrup.

flax
A NUTRITION POWERHOUSE

One of the pleasures of travelling through southern Saskatchewan in early summer is the breathtaking sight of flax fields in bloom. The flax plant's distinctive periwinkle blue flowers make each field look like an ocean in the middle of the prairie—I am in awe every time I see it!

After several weeks of flowering, each delicate blue flax flower will drop its petals to expose a single tiny capsule. Under the heat of the prairie sun, the pod will slowly mature, become dry, and begin to split. Hidden inside will be a powerful collection of glossy golden or dark brown flax seeds rich in soluble and insoluble dietary fibre, polyunsaturated oils, Omega-3 fatty acids, protein, vitamins, minerals, and phytonutrients.

Flax was first grown in Saskatchewan in the early 1900s, and since then the province has become Canada's leading producer, accounting for 70% of all Canadian production and 25% of world production. Not only is flax vital nutritionally, the entire plant is useful. Fibre from the stems can be spun into linen and into canvas bags and fishing nets. Various parts of the plant can be used to make dyes, paper, medicine, and cosmetics, as well as wood finishing and paint products. Flax is even grown as an ornamental plant in home gardens. Some farmers bale what's left over from harvesting and sell it to home builders who wish to use an eco-conscious alternative to insulate new homes.

Flax seed is very hard and must be ground for the body to profit from all its nutrients. Grind the seeds just before you use them and refrigerate any unused portion to keep it from going rancid. Flax oil is a nutritious edible oil that is delicious in your morning smoothie. Don't heat flax oil; just drizzle it on your dishes after they are cooked. Ground flax can be used as an excellent binder in meat loaf or hamburger patties. And its nutty flavour is super in muffins, cakes, and bread. Go ahead...experiment. Your body...and your heart...will thank you.

Wayne Hart's flax crop, near Condie Nature Refuge northwest of Regina, SK.

FACING PAGE, TOP: Flax harvest.

FACING PAGE, BOTTOM: Flax in bloom.

ABOVE: Flax stems laden with tiny, dry capsules about to split with flax seed.

143

Oatmeal-Raisin Bread

This nourishing bread uses prairie oats and flax. It's not too sweet. We enjoy this bread any time of the day: in the morning toasted with butter, at lunch with a bowl of stick-to-your-ribs soup, or at dinner instead of potatoes.

MAKES 3 ROUND LOAVES

1 cup (250 mL) **large-flake rolled oats** (old-fashioned)

1/4 cup (60 mL) **flax seeds**

1 cup (250 mL) **golden raisins**

1 cup (250 mL) **boiling water**

1 tbsp (15 mL) **traditional active dry yeast**

1 cup (250 mL) **lukewarm water** (first amount)

about 4 1/2 cups (1125 mL) **unbleached all-purpose flour**

1 cup (250 mL) **whole wheat flour**

1 1/2 tbsp (22 mL) **kosher salt**

3 tbsp (45 mL) **liquid honey**

1 cup (250 mL) **lukewarm water** (second amount)

In a large bowl, combine the oats, flax seeds, and raisins. Add the boiling water. Stir and let stand about 30 minutes, or until lukewarm.

In a small bowl, add the yeast to 1 cup (250 mL) lukewarm water. The water should be no warmer than a newborn baby's bath. Let it stand for 10 minutes, until the yeast has bubbled up. If the yeast has not bubbled up, it is dead and needs replacing.

In a large mixer bowl, combine 4 cups (1 L) all-purpose flour, whole wheat flour, and salt. Stir with a wooden spoon to combine.

Stir the yeast, and add it to the lukewarm oat mixture. Add the honey and 1 cup (250 mL) lukewarm water and stir well. Add to the flour mixture and stir with a wooden spoon to combine.

Fit the mixer with a dough hook and knead the dough at speed #2 for 5 minutes (or on the very lowest speed for 10 minutes), adding additional flour a spoonful at a time until the dough cleans the sides of the bowl. The dough should be slightly sticky. (Alternatively, knead the dough by hand on a lightly floured counter for 10 minutes.)

Remove the dough. Lightly grease the bowl with about 2 tsp (10 mL) oil and place dough back in the work bowl. Turn the dough to completely coat it with the oil. Place the bowl into a plastic bag and let it rise at room temperature for 1 1/2 hours, or until double in size.

Once the dough has risen, remove the bowl from the bag and punch the dough down. (At this point, you can refrigerate the dough until ready to form. Covered, it will last several days in the refrigerator. Bring the dough to room temperature before proceeding with the recipe.)

Knead the dough several times on an unfloured counter. Invert the mixing bowl and place it over the dough for 10 minutes to allow the dough to relax.

Meanwhile, preheat oven to 400°F (200°C). If you have one, place a pizza stone in the bottom third of the oven to preheat.

Using a bench scraper or sharp knife, cut the dough into three equal pieces. Knead each piece into a ball and transfer dough to three greased 8-inch (20 cm) round cake tins. Cover and let rise 30 to 40 minutes.

Dust the risen loaves lightly with flour and gently rub the flour over the loaves. Cut several slits in the top of each loaf about ¹/₄-inch (5 mm) deep. Place the bread pans in the oven directly on the pizza stone, if using.

Place a pan with 2 cups (500 mL) of water in the oven to create a moist heat.

Bake for 40 minutes. Cover the loaves with a sheet of foil if they begin to brown too much. Remove the loaves from the pans and place them on a wire rack to cool.

Oats near harvest time, south of Prince Albert, SK.

Whole Wheat-Quinoa Bread

This hearty bread is filled with all the goodness of the prairies: quinoa, spelt, and stone-ground whole wheat flour. Spelt flakes are available at health food stores.

MAKES 3 ROUND LOAVES

1 tbsp (15 mL) **traditional active dry yeast**

3 cups (750 mL) **lukewarm water**, divided

about 4 cups (1 L) **unbleached all-purpose flour**

2 cups (500 mL) **stone-ground whole wheat flour**

1 cup (250 mL) **cooked quinoa**, red or white (see sidebar)

1 cup (250 mL) **spelt flakes**, or wheat flakes

1 1/2 tbsp (22 mL) **kosher salt**

In a small bowl, add the yeast to 1 cup (250 mL) lukewarm water. The water should be no warmer than a newborn baby's bath. Let it stand for 10 minutes, until the yeast has bubbled up. If the yeast has not bubbled up, it is dead and needs replacing.

In a large mixer bowl, combine 3 cups (750 mL) unbleached all-purpose flour, whole wheat flour, cooked quinoa, spelt flakes, and salt. Stir with a wooden spoon to combine.

Stir the proofed yeast and add it to the flour mixture along with the remaining 2 cups (500 mL) lukewarm water. Stir with a wooden spoon to combine.

Fit the mixer with a dough hook and knead the dough at speed #2 for 5 minutes (or on the very lowest speed for 10 minutes), adding additional flour one spoonful at a time until the dough cleans the sides of the bowl. The dough should be slightly sticky.

Remove dough. Lightly grease the work bowl with about 2 tsp (10 mL) oil. Return the dough, then turn it over in the bowl to coat it with the oil. Place the bowl in a plastic bag and let the dough rise at room temperature for 1 1/2 hours, or until double in size.

When the dough has risen, remove the bowl from the bag and punch the dough down. (At this point, you can refrigerate the dough until ready to form into loaves. Covered, it will last several days in the refrigerator. Bring the dough to room temperature before proceeding with the recipe.)

Knead the dough several times on an unfloured counter. Invert the mixing bowl and place it over the dough for 10 minutes to allow the dough to relax.

Using a bench scraper or sharp knife, cut dough into three equal pieces. Knead each piece into a ball and transfer the dough to three greased 8-inch (20 cm) round cake tins. Cover and let the dough rise for 30 to 40 minutes.

Meanwhile, preheat the oven to 400°F (200°C). If you have one, place a pizza stone in the bottom third of the oven to preheat.

Dust the risen loaves lightly with flour and gently rub the flour over the loaves. Cut several slits in the top of each loaf about 1/4-inch (5 mm) deep. Place the bread pans in the oven. If using a pizza stone, place the pans directly onto the hot stone.

Place a pan with 2 cups (500 mL) of water on a rack in the oven to create a moist heat. This helps to make a nice crispy crust on the loaf.

Bake for 40 minutes. If the loaves begin to brown too much, lightly set a sheet of foil on them. Remove the loaves immediately from the cake tins and place them on a wire rack to cool.

Cooking Quinoa

I often cook up a large batch of quinoa for use in salads and to make this bread. Unlike rice, which doubles in volume when cooked, quinoa triples in volume. If you want to make just enough quinoa for this recipe, rinse 1/3 cup (80 mL) quinoa for 3 minutes under cold running water. Add it to a pot with 2/3 cup (160 mL) boiling lightly salted water. Cover and simmer on low heat until cooked, about 20 minutes. Fluff with a fork and let cool completely.

Spelt Cookies

Cookie lovers will never guess that these are healthy. Spelt flakes and hemp hearts can be found at health food stores. Hemp hearts are also called hemp seeds.

MAKES ABOUT 3 DOZEN COOKIES

¹/₂ cup (125 mL) **stone-ground whole wheat flour**

³/₄ cup (185 mL) **unbleached all-purpose flour**

¹/₂ tsp (2 mL) **baking soda**

¹/₂ tsp (2 mL) **kosher salt**

¹/₂ tsp (2 mL) **ground cinnamon**, optional

1 cup (250 mL) **spelt flakes** or wheat flakes

¹/₄ cup (60 mL) **hemp hearts**

³/₄ cup (185 mL) **unsalted butter**, room temperature

1¹/₄ cup (300 mL) packed **brown sugar**

1 **egg**

1 tsp (5 mL) **pure vanilla extract**

¹/₂ cup (125 mL) **semi-sweet chocolate chips**

¹/₂ cup (125 mL) **raisins**

Preheat oven to 375°F (190°C). Line two cookie sheets with parchment paper.

Scoop the whole wheat flour and the all-purpose flour gently into the measuring cups. Level the top with the flat edge of a knife. Transfer the flour to a medium bowl and add the baking soda, salt, cinnamon, spelt flakes, and hemp hearts. Stir to mix and set aside.

In a large mixer bowl, beat the butter and brown sugar together until light and fluffy. Add the egg and beat well. Add the vanilla. Add the flour-spelt mixture all at once; stir on low speed until just combined.

With a wooden spoon, stir in the chocolate chips and raisins.

Roll the dough into balls about the size of a golf ball and set on a cookie sheet, spacing each ball about 2 inches (5 cm) apart. Flatten each ball with a fork or the underside of a water glass.

Bake about 18 minutes. Remove from the oven, and let the baked cookies cool about 10 minutes before removing them to a rack. Cookies should be soft and chewy when cool.

Apple Butter

"Delicious" is the word to describe this tasty apple butter. Spread it on toast or get creative and use it as the main ingredient in a great barbeque sauce. The apples cook for about 15 hours, a process that can easily be done while you sleep.

MAKES ABOUT 4 PINTS (1 L)

15 large **apples**, peeled and cored

2 cups (500 mL) **granulated sugar**

2 tsp (10 mL) **ground cinnamon**

$^1/_4$ tsp (1 mL) **ground cloves**

$^1/_4$ tsp (1 mL) **kosher salt**

Preheat oven to 300°F (150°C).

Cut the peeled and cored apples into quarters. Working in batches, finely chop the apples in a food processor. Transfer to a large bowl.

When all the apples are finely chopped, add the sugar, cinnamon, cloves, and salt. Mix well.

Transfer the mixture to a lightly greased crock-pot or casserole dish. Cover and place the pot in the preheated oven for one hour. Reduce heat to 250°F (120°C) and let the apples cook for about 15 hours.

Remove the lid and stir the apples. Let the mixture continue to cook, uncovered, until very thick. The mixture will be dark. This step could take another three to six hours depending on how juicy the apples are.

When the mixture is very thick and dark, remove the crock-pot from the oven and let it cool.

Using a hand immersion blender or stand blender, purée the apple mixture until silky smooth.

Transfer the mixture to glass jars or plastic containers, leaving about $^1/_2$-inch (1.5 cm) head space. Seal with a lid. Freeze for up to one year, or refrigerate for up to one month.

Dry, the frozen prairie fields sleep,

Heavily clad anglers jig for fish on frozen ice,

Deer in their heavy coats paw the prairie snow for grass,

Laughing children sled and slide in the crisp outdoor air.

Jelly jars bring forth delicious tastes of summer's past.

Rich stews slowly braise, warm loaves await the first bite,

Festive meals decked in their fullest finery bring loved ones close...

The time to celebrate.

The time to recharge.

Highbush cranberries in my backyard.

winter

Mushroom-Barley Soup

After wheat, barley is the second most widely grown cereal crop in Canada, with most of the production centered in Saskatchewan, Alberta, and Manitoba. The majority of the crop goes to animal feed and to malting, where it's fermented to fill your glass with tasty beer. Pearl barley has had the hull and bran removed to make it edible for human consumption. Pearl barley finds its way into hearty soups and pilafs. This soup will keep you satisfied all afternoon. Enjoy it with Oatmeal-Raisin Bread (recipe on page 144).

SERVES 6 TO 8

³/₄ cup (185 mL) **pearl barley**, rinsed

13 cups (3.25 L) **chicken**, beef, or vegetable **stock**

2 **carrots**, peeled and coarsely diced

2 stalks **celery**, peeled and coarsely diced

3 cups (750 mL) sliced **fresh mushrooms**

¹/₄ cup (60 mL) finely chopped **fresh dill**

salt and **pepper**, to taste

Cook pearl barley in 3 cups (750 mL) chicken stock for about 40 minutes, or until fully cooked. Set aside.

In a large stockpot, bring to a simmer 10 cups (2.5 L) chicken stock. Add the diced carrots and celery, cooked barley, and mushrooms. Let simmer 15 minutes, or until the vegetables are tender. Add fresh dill, salt, and pepper to taste.

Saskatchewan Soup

What better name for a soup filled with hearty Saskatchewan ingredients—
chickpeas, wild rice, lentils, and garden vegetables. Enjoy a bowl with fresh
whole-grain bread.

SERVES 6 TO 8 GENEROUSLY

A field of wheat just
weeks from harvest,
Stoney Beach, SK.

1 can (19 oz/540 mL) **diced tomatoes**

¹/₂ cup (125 mL) washed **wild rice**

¹/₂ cup (125 mL) **small whole lentils**,
red or brown (do not use split lentils)*

1 can (19 oz/540 mL) **chickpeas**, drained
and rinsed well

1 large **onion**, diced, about 1 ¹/₂ cups
(375 ml)

1 **bay leaf**

1 tsp (5 mL) **dried summer savoury
leaves**, lightly crushed

16 cups (4 L) **chicken**, beef,
or vegetable **stock**

1 cup (250 mL) **frozen peas**

1 cup (250 mL) **frozen corn niblets**

1 cup (250 mL) **cooked spaghetti
noodles**, cut into 2-inch (5 cm) lengths**

3 tbsp (45 mL) finely sliced **fresh basil
leaves**

salt and **pepper**, to taste

In a large stockpot, combine the diced tomatoes, wild rice, whole lentils, chickpeas,
diced onion, bay leaf, dried summer savoury leaves, and stock. Bring to a boil.
Reduce heat and simmer, uncovered, for 2 hours.

About 30 minutes before serving, add the peas, corn, and cooked spaghetti.
Stir and continue to simmer soup. Just before serving, stir in the fresh basil.
Add salt and pepper, to taste.

* Large whole green or brown lentils can also be used, although the texture of the soup is
more appealing with the small whole lentils.

**Uncooked noodles can also be added. Break the strands into 2-inch (5 cm) lengths
and measure out ¹/₂ cup (125 ml). Add to the soup 1 hour before serving.

Split Pea Soup

On a winter day, nothing could be more comforting than homemade soup. This hearty soup hits the spot perfectly. Serve it with a thick slice of Whole Wheat-Quinoa Bread (recipe on page 147).

SERVES 10 TO 12

2 large or 3 medium **carrots**, diced

1 large **onion**, diced

2 stalks **celery**, diced

1 lb (454 g) **dried split green** or yellow **peas**, rinsed

1 **bay leaf**

2 to 3 oz (56 to 85 g) **cooked ham**, or smoked turkey or all-beef salami, diced to ¼ inch (5 mm)

1½ tsp (7 mL) **dried thyme**

12 cups (3 L) **homemade chicken** or vegetable **stock**

salt and **pepper**, to taste

In a large stockpot, combine all the ingredients. Bring to a boil and simmer 2 to 2½ hours, or until peas are very soft. Add more water or stock if the soup is too thick. Season with salt and pepper. Taste and adjust seasonings.

Red Lentil Soup

Since split red lentils fall apart and become soft as they cook, they are lovely for creating a soup that has a creamy texture. The cumin gives this soup a deep exotic flavour.

SERVES 6

2 tbsp (30 mL) **olive oil** or vegetable oil

1 **onion**, diced

2 cloves **garlic**, finely chopped

2 stalks **celery**, diced

1 tsp (5 mL) **turmeric powder**

2 tsp (10 mL) **ground cumin**

1 **cinnamon stick**

$^1/_2$ tsp (2 mL) freshly ground **black pepper**

1 cup (250 mL) rinsed **split red lentils**

1 cup (250 mL) canned **diced tomatoes**

4 cups (1 L) **chicken** or vegetable **stock**

kosher salt, to taste

2 small sprigs of **cilantro**, for garnish

$^1/_3$ cup (80 mL) **plain yogurt**, for garnish

In a Dutch oven or large pot, heat the oil over medium-low heat. Sauté the onion and garlic for several minutes. Add the celery, season the mixture with salt, and sauté another 3 to 4 minutes.

Add the turmeric, cumin, cinnamon stick and black pepper and stir constantly for one minute to toast the spices.

Add the lentils, tomatoes, and stock. Bring to a boil and simmer, partially covered, for 50 to 60 minutes.

Serve as is, or purée. Taste and adjust seasonings.

Ladle into bowls and garnish with a dollop of yogurt and a sprig of cilantro.

lentils
HUMBLE GIANT
∙∙∙∙∙∙∙∙∙∙∙∙∙∙∙∙∙∙∙∙∙

Never judge a book by its cover, or a food by its name. A long-time staple of Indian and Middle Eastern cooking, that little, unassuming green lentil on your plate is steeped in history and packed with nutrition.

Evidence of lentils has been dated as far back as 11,000 BCE to the Franchthi Cave in Greece. In the Bible (Genesis 25: 29-34), Esau gave away his birthright for a bowl of red lentil stew. And Saskatchewan, too, has its own lentil history, one that continues to have a profound and worldwide impact.

In the early 1970s, perhaps 500 acres of lentils were grown in Saskatchewan. During the decade that followed, research at the University of Saskatchewan led to the development of two important lentil varieties: the Laird (large green) in 1978 and the Eston (small green) in 1980. Canada has since become a major exporter of lentils, with the Laird green lentil the most widely grown and recognized lentil variety in the world. In 2008,

Canada surpassed India as the top lentil-producing country. And of that crop, Saskatchewan produces 99%!

Lentils are a nutrition giant, an excellent source of fibre and protein, as well as vitamins and trace minerals. They are inexpensive and simple to cook. Whether green, or brown, or red, or black, lentils can be cooked without presoaking and are ready to eat in no time. Go ahead and create a hearty chili or a spicy curry; try them as a pilaf or as a base for vegetarian burgers; toss some into your salad. Do try sprouting them for a highly nutritious addition to sandwiches and salads, or puréeing them to make cakes and cookies. Flour ground from lentils is gluten-free. When cooking with lentils, the options are endless and the nutritional benefits are huge.

FACING PAGE: Organic farmer David Tanner harvests lentils outside Regina, SK.

ABOVE: (left to right) beluga, small brown, split red, and large green lentils.

Braised Lentils

This comfy side dish is perfect for blustery winter days. Serve it with your favourite meat, chicken, or fish dish.

SERVES 4 TO 6

1 cup (250 mL) **whole lentils**, brown or green (not the split red variety)

1 tbsp (15 mL) **vegetable oil**

half a medium **cooking onion**, chopped

1 **tomato**, diced

1 tbsp (15 mL) chopped **fresh basil leaves**, or 1 tsp (5 mL) dried basil

1 ¹/₂ cups (375 mL) **chicken** or vegetable **stock**

Rinse the lentils and remove any stones. Set aside.

In a medium saucepan over medium heat, sauté the chopped onion in the oil until translucent. Add the diced tomato, basil, and lentils. Add the chicken stock. Bring to a boil, and simmer about 15 to 20 minutes, or until the lentils are soft and begin to split. Season with salt and pepper. Serve hot.

Squash Bake

This simple recipe uses a small amount of brown sugar and spices to make it a vegetable side dish rather than a dessert. Serve it with grilled or roasted poultry. You might want to experiment with different squashes, such as acorn or delicata.

SERVES 6 TO 8

1 large **butternut squash**

2 large **sweet potatoes**

1 ¹/₂ tbsp (22 mL) **brown sugar**

¹/₄ tsp (1 mL) *each* **ground cinnamon**, **ground nutmeg**, and **salt**

freshly ground **black pepper**, to taste

1 ¹/₂ tbsp (22 mL) **melted butter**

Preheat oven to 375°F (190°C).

Peel squash and sweet potatoes. Remove seeds from squash.

Cut vegetables into ³/₄-inch (2 cm) cubes and place in an oiled 9- × 13-inch (3.5 L) lasagne pan or shallow oven-proof dish. Sprinkle with brown sugar, cinnamon, nutmeg, salt, and pepper. Drizzle with melted butter.

Cover with foil and bake for 45 minutes. Remove foil and continue to bake another 30 minutes, until the vegetables are very soft and browned. Serve warm.

Turkey (or Chicken) and Barley Salad

This salad is a healthy option for using up leftover turkey or roast chicken. It is delicious with a slice of Granola Bâtard (recipe on page 44).

SERVES 6 AS A MAIN COURSE

1 cup (250 mL) **pearl barley**, rinsed

2 cups (500 mL) **water**

$^1/_2$ tsp (2 mL) **kosher salt**

2 to 3 cups (500 to 750 mL) leftover **roast turkey** or **roast chicken**, torn into bite-size pieces

1 cup (250 mL) canned **black beans**, rinsed and drained

1 cup (250 mL) **corn niblets**, frozen or fresh

1 **red pepper**, diced

1 cup (250 mL) **dried cranberries**

2 **green onions**, trimmed and thinly sliced on the diagonal

3 tbsp (45 mL) finely chopped **fresh basil**

3 tbsp (45 mL) finely chopped **fresh cilantro**

$^1/_2$ cup (125 mL) **toasted slivered almonds** or pine nuts

DRESSING

3 tbsp (45 mL) **red wine vinegar**

1 tsp (5 mL) **maple syrup**

1 clove **garlic**, minced

1 tsp (5 mL) **Dijon mustard**

5 tbsp (75 mL) **extra virgin olive oil**

salt and **pepper**, to taste

In a medium saucepan, bring the water to a boil. Add the barley and salt and cook until al dente. Set aside to cool.

In a large bowl, combine the turkey or chicken with the cooled barley, rinsed black beans, corn, red pepper, dried cranberries, green onions, basil, cilantro, and toasted nuts.

To make the dressing, in a small bowl, whisk together the red wine vinegar, maple syrup, minced garlic, and Dijon mustard. Slowly whisk in the olive oil; season with salt and pepper. Pour over the salad and toss to coat.

Serve with crusty whole grain bread.

Sun-Dried Tomato and Basil Mashed Potatoes

This is comfort food taken up a notch. I first tasted these mashed potatoes at a Regina steakhouse, where they had been prepared by Chef Thomas Rush. They were delicious. The next day I tried to duplicate their incredible flavour. I think that this recipe comes very close. During the winter, when fresh basil is scarce, I tinker and add about 1 to 2 tsp (5 to 10 mL) basil pesto in place of the fresh herbs. You can make this recipe with peeled or unpeeled red potatoes. The cooked potato skins add not only a nutritional boost but also some interesting texture and colour to the dish. Enjoy these potatoes with steak, sausages, chicken, or fish, such as Smoked Steelhead Trout (recipe on page 76).

SERVES 6 TO 8

Red-skinned potatoes from Lincoln Gardens, Lumsden, at Regina Farmers' Market.

6 medium **Klondike Rose** (red) **potatoes**

1 tbsp (15 mL) **butter**

milk, as needed

salt and **pepper**, to taste

¹/₄ cup (60 mL) **sun-dried tomatoes**, packed in oil, chopped

¹/₄ cup (60 mL) **fresh basil leaves**, thinly sliced

If the potatoes are new and their skins unblemished, there is no need to peel them. Quarter or halve the potatoes; boil in lightly salted water until the potatoes are tender and fully cooked. Remove from heat. Drain and let the potatoes stand without a lid for one minute to allow any water to evaporate.

Add the butter to the pot. Mash the potatoes with a potato masher until no lumps remain. Add a small amount of milk, if required, to make a mixture that is silky but firm when scooped. Do not overmix or the potatoes will become gluey.

Add the sun-dried tomatoes, fresh basil, salt and pepper. Stir with a wooden spoon to combine. Taste and adjust the seasonings; add more basil if necessary. Serve hot.

Mary's Marinated Beets

This is a terrific side dish that gets its sweetness from the beets but a zesty kick from the garlic. This recipe comes from Mary Woloshyn in Regina, whom I interviewed several years ago for an article I wrote on Ukrainian Christmas.

MAKES 2 TO 3 CUPS (500 TO 750 ML)

4 to 5 medium or large cooked **whole beets** (fresh or canned)

1 tbsp (15 mL) **soy sauce**

1 tbsp (15 mL) **white** or malt **vinegar**

1 tbsp (15 mL) **granulated sugar**

1 tbsp (15 mL) **vegetable oil**

2 cloves **garlic**, minced

salt and **pepper**, to taste

Julienne the beets into 1 × ¼-inch (2.5 × .5 cm) matchsticks. Place into a bowl together with the soy sauce, vinegar, granulated sugar, oil, garlic, salt, and pepper. Combine well. Let the beets marinate in the refrigerator for 1 to 2 hours. These beets will keep for at least one week.

Smoky Chipotle Hummus

Canada is the leading exporter of chickpeas. Most are shipped to Spain, India, and Pakistan. Saskatchewan produces a whopping 99% of Canadian production. This hummus recipe is zipped up with chipotle peppers and cilantro.

MAKES ABOUT 2 CUPS (500 ML)

1 can (19 oz/540 mL) **chickpeas**, drained and rinsed well

¹/₃ cup (80 mL) **tahini paste**

juice of 1 lemon, or more if desired

2 tbsp (30 mL) **extra virgin olive oil**

1 **chipotle pepper** with adobo sauce, or to taste

1 large clove **garlic**, coarsely chopped

1 tsp (5 mL) **ground cumin**

pinch **kosher salt**

water, as required

¹/₃ cup (80 mL) chopped **fresh cilantro**

In a food processor, process the chickpeas, tahini paste, lemon juice, olive oil, chipotle pepper, garlic, cumin, and salt. Blend to a smooth paste, adding small amounts of water as necessary to make a thick paste. Be careful not to make the dip too thin. Taste and adjust seasonings. Transfer to a bowl and stir in the cilantro.

Serve with wedges of fresh pita bread or a variety of fresh vegetables.

Beets grown by Lincoln Gardens, Lumsden, displayed at the Regina Farmers' Market.

Baba Ganoush

This classic Mediterranean dip is so very simple to whip together. It's scrumptious with crunchy vegetables, fresh pita bread, and chickpea falafel. Sesame seeds are to tahini paste as peanuts are to peanut butter. Tahini is the paste made from ground sesame seeds. It can be found in the international food section of large supermarkets or in health food stores.

MAKES ABOUT 2 CUPS (500 ML)

1 large or 2 small **eggplants**

vegetable oil, for brushing

salt and **pepper**, to taste

¼ cup (60 mL) **tahini paste**

3 cloves **garlic**, halved

juice of 1 lemon

1 tsp (5 mL) **ground cumin**

1 tsp (5 mL) **ground coriander**

pinch **kosher salt**

1 tbsp (15 mL) **extra virgin olive oil**

1 tbsp (15 mL) finely chopped **fresh cilantro leaves**

Preheat barbeque to high.*

Cut each eggplant in half lengthwise. Brush the fleshy side with oil and sprinkle with salt and pepper. Place cut side down on the grill and barbeque, turning the eggplant halves occasionally, until charred and very soft. Set aside to cool.

When the cooked eggplant is cool enough to handle, scrape the flesh and seeds into a food processor bowl; discard the skin and stem. Add tahini paste, garlic cloves, lemon juice, cumin, coriander, salt, and olive oil. Pulse until the mixture is combined. You can either purée it or leave it chunky. Scrape into a bowl and stir in the chopped cilantro leaves. Taste and adjust seasonings.

The eggplants can also be baked in the oven. Preheat oven to 450°F (235°C). With a sharp knife, make several slits in the eggplant to allow steam to escape while baking. Place the whole eggplant on a parchment paper–lined baking sheet; bake about 40 minutes, or until very soft and the skin is shriveled. Remove from the oven and cut open each eggplant to allow the hot steam to escape before scraping out the flesh and seeds.

Prairie Spices

Canada's spice production is centered in Western Canada, primarily in Saskatchewan. Two major spice crops are caraway and coriander but anise, cumin, dill, and fenugreek are also grown. Sadly, these spices don't typically show up at farmers' markets because most production is farmed for commercial sale. But next time you're in the grocery store, remember that the ingredients in those little jars that line the spice aisle were grown on Canada's sunny prairies.

Cowboy Beef Pie and Turnovers

This is a great recipe for batch cooking. Bake a pie for supper and freeze the turnovers for lunch boxes.

MAKES ONE 8-INCH (20 CM) PIE AND ABOUT 6 TURNOVERS

FILLING

Make Ahead Tip

The turnovers and pie can be frozen either before or after baking. To bake frozen unbaked turnovers, add an additional 5 minutes to the baking time. To bake frozen unbaked pie, add an additional 10 to 15 minutes to the baking time.

1 lb (454 g) **top sirloin beef**

1 **cooking onion**

1 large **carrot**, peeled

1 medium **potato**, peeled

2 cloves **garlic**, finely chopped

1 tbsp (15 mL) **vegetable oil**

$^1/_2$ cup (125 mL) **dry red wine** or beef broth

$^1/_2$ lb (227 g) **mushrooms**, finely chopped

$^1/_2$ cup (125 mL) **green peas**, fresh or frozen

2 tsp (10 mL) **dried thyme**, or 2 tbsp (30 mL) fresh thyme leaves

2 **fresh tomatoes**, diced

$^1/_4$ cup (60 mL) chopped **fresh parsley**

salt and **pepper**, to taste

2 recipes **Basic Flaky Pastry** (recipe on page 86)

2 **eggs**, beaten

For easier cutting, freeze the sirloin for about 1 hour, until about half frozen. Trim the beef of any fat. Cut the beef into $^1/_2$-inch (1.5 cm) cubes. Dice the cooking onion, carrot and potato into $^1/_2$-inch (1.5 cm) cubes.

In a large sauté pan, heat the oil over medium heat. Add the onion, carrot, potato, and garlic. Season with salt and pepper. Cook over medium heat until the onion is translucent. Remove the vegetables to a bowl.

Add additional oil to the pan and brown the beef. Return the cooked vegetables to the pan. Add the red wine, mushrooms, green peas, thyme, and tomatoes. Simmer gently over medium heat, uncovered, about 20 minutes or until the sauce is reduced and thickened. (Do not cook down until the filling is dry. It should be moist, similar to a stew.) Season with salt and pepper, to taste, and add fresh parsley. Cool completely.

Preheat oven to 425°F (220°C).

Divide the prepared pastry in half.

TURNOVERS: Line a baking sheet with parchment paper. Set aside.

To make the turnovers, use one half of the pastry. Roll out pastry, and cut into six 6-inch (15 cm) rounds. Place about 2 tbsp (30 mL) of the filling in the centre of each round. Fold over pastry and pinch edges closed with your fingers. With a paring knife, make a small slit on the top of the turnover and brush with the beaten egg.

Place the turnovers on the baking sheet. Bake for 15 minutes. Lower heat to 350°F (180°C) and bake another 10 to 12 minutes. Cool.

PIE: To make the pie, divide the remaining ball of pastry into two equal balls. Roll out one ball to a 10-inch (25.5 cm) circle, large enough to line an 8-inch (20 cm) pie plate. Transfer the pastry to the pie plate, gently easing the pastry into place. Do not tug or pull the pastry. Trim the edges. Roll out the remaining ball to a 10-inch (25.5 cm) circle. Set aside.

Add the remaining beef filling (about half) to the lined pie plate and cover with the additional pastry. Seal the edges with your fingers and trim. With the tip of a sharp knife, make slits on top. Brush with beaten egg. Bake for 15 minutes at 425°F (220°C) and then another 30 minutes at 350°F (180°C).

beef
A CANADIAN TRADITION

The "cowboy way" is still strong on the Canadian prairie. Vast cattle ranches rich in a sea of native grasses support massive herds of beef. Ranchers clad with felt Stetsons, faded Wranglers, leather chaps, and cowboy boots still rope and corral the herd on horseback.

After Alberta, Saskatchewan is Canada's second-largest beef-producing province. Most of the province's cattle ranchers raise purebred or crossbred Angus, Hereford, Charolais, or Simmental. Some ranchers supply to niche markets with exotic breeds, organic beef, or grass-fed beef. Cattle are bred to produce well-marbled, tender, and flavourful meat.

Beef is an excellent source of protein, iron, zinc, and vitamin B_{12}. Tender cuts such as the prime rib roast, tenderloin, and rib-eye steak are delicious seasoned with salt and pepper, or steak spice, and grilled to desired doneness. Some less-tender cuts, such as the rump roast or the meaty rib roast, are superb when braised long-and-slow with tomatoes, herbs, and beef stock; others, such as the flank steak, are fabulous when grilled to medium and sliced across the grain on the diagonal. And finally, who can argue with a classic hamburger dressed to the nines? Canadian beef is easy to find and easy to prepare. A convenient, nutritious, and delicious source of protein, it connects us to the land and to our history.

CLOCKWISE FROM TOP LEFT:

Black and Red Angus cattle at Hextall Livestock, Grenfell, SK.

Butcher Jeff Fritzsche, Butcher Boy Meats (Park St.), Regina, SK.

Black Angus-Hereford cross at Hextall Livestock.

Beef Jerky ready for the smoker.

Prime rib roast.

169

Asian Short Ribs

Asian-style short ribs are a lesser-known cut of meat. Have your local butcher custom-cut them for you. These ribs are crosscut into ¹/₂-inch (1.5 cm) thick slices from a four-rib rack of beef short ribs. Don't have them cut thicker than this or they will be tough. The beauty of these ribs is they take only about six minutes to cook from the time they hit the grill.

SERVES 4 TO 6

¹/₃ cup (80 mL) **kecap manis***
or soy sauce

¹/₄ cup (60 mL) **liquid honey**

2 tbsp (30 mL) **Asian sesame oil**

3 cloves **garlic**, minced

2 tbsp (30 mL) **rice wine vinegar**

1 tsp (5 mL) **powdered Chinese 5-spice**
or grated fresh ginger

pinch **chili flakes**

2 lbs (907 g) **Asian short ribs**

sesame seeds, for garnish

In a small bowl, whisk together the kecap manis or soy sauce, liquid honey, sesame oil, minced garlic, rice wine vinegar, Chinese 5-spice, and chili flakes. Set aside.

Place the short ribs in a plastic zip-lock bag. Add the sauce. Seal the bag and toss well to coat the ribs. Let marinate for several hours or overnight in the refrigerator.

Preheat barbeque to high. Grill the ribs, about 3 minutes per side. Remove to a platter and sprinkle with sesame seeds.

These ribs can also be fried on the stove in a grill pan, or broiled in the oven.

* Kecap manis, a thick soy sauce, can be found at Asian grocery stores. It is becoming more available at larger supermarkets that specialize in Asian groceries.

Wintertime Shore Lunch

If you are a winter angler, try this shore lunch recipe for breaded fish and skillet potatoes. If you don't have a favourite barbeque rub, use one of the rubs from pages 21, 74, 76, or 77. Precook the potatoes, and assemble and package the ingredients at home before you head out into the great outdoors.

SERVES 4

fresh-caught **filleted fish**

FISH BREADING

¹/₂ cup (125 mL) **flour**

¹/₂ cup (125 mL) **cornstarch**

¹/₂ cup (125 mL) **cornmeal**

¹/₂ cup (125 mL) your favourite **barbeque rub**

1 beaten **egg**

1 cup (250 mL) **milk** or beer

SKILLET POTATOES

1 lb (454 g) cooked whole red or white **baby potatoes**

3 tbsp (45 mL) **olive oil**

juice of 1 lemon

1 clove **garlic**, minced

handful chopped **fresh dill**

1 bottle **vegetable oil**, for frying

lemon wedges, precut

coleslaw, homemade or purchased

For cooking your shore lunch, take along 2 large cast-iron skillets, a set of tongs, 1 or 2 metal spatulas, and a set of oven mitts or heavy gloves.

Don't forget to bag your garbage and take it with you when you leave. And never leave an open fire, even if it's on ice. Kick lots of snow over the fire to completely extinguish any embers.

BEFORE YOU LEAVE: Combine the flour, cornstarch, cornmeal, and barbeque rub in a large zip-lock bag. Seal.

Pour the beaten egg into a medium plastic container with a lid. You will be dipping the fish fillets into this container, so choose one of an appropriate size. If using milk, add the milk as well and seal. (If you are using beer, take the beer separately and add it to the egg just before using.)

Combine the olive oil, lemon juice, and garlic in a small container with a lid. Seal. Place the chopped dill in a small zip-lock bag.

FISH: Place a large cast-iron skillet over the hot coals of an open fire. Add oil to cover the bottom of the skillet.

Using tongs, dip the freshly filleted fish into the milk-egg (or beer-egg) mixture and then into the breading. Toss to coat. Fry in a medium-hot pan for several minutes per side.

SKILLET POTATOES: In the second skillet, heat the pre-cooked potatoes in oil. Cook until the potatoes are golden brown and the skin is just starting to crisp slightly. Just before serving, pour the oil-lemon mixture over the potatoes. Be careful not to spill the mixture in the hot coals. Toss and add the chopped dill. Serve alongside the warm fish fillets. Serve with lemon wedges and coleslaw.

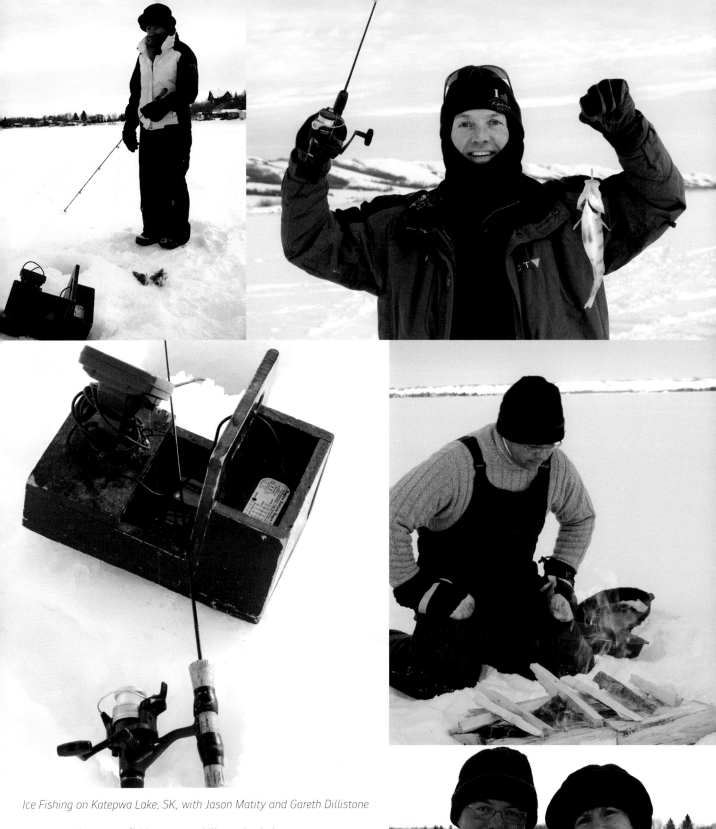

Ice Fishing on Katepwa Lake, SK, with Jason Matity and Gareth Dillistone

FACING PAGE: Jason, our fishing expert, drills our ice hole.

ABOVE, CLOCKWISE FROM TOP LEFT: I found that jigging for perch was tremendously relaxing; Gareth displays his catch of the day; Jason preps the fire for a fabulous shore lunch; Jason and I show off one of my catches—a lovely perch; we used this fish finder to help us decide where to drill through the ice.

173

White Fish in Coconut Curry Sauce

Walleye, pike, or bass are delicious when gently poached in this exotic and deeply flavoured sauce. Adjust the quantity of red chili peppers to your desired "heat" level.

SERVES 6

2 lbs (907 g) **fish fillets**, skin off, ideally firm-fleshed white fish such as walleye, pike, or bass

1 large or 2 small cloves **garlic**, chopped

1 inch (2.5 cm) **gingerroot**, peeled and julienned into thin strips

1 tsp (5 mL) **turmeric powder**

2 small **Thai red chili peppers**, finely sliced, or 1/4 tsp (1 mL) dried chili flakes

1 tbsp (15 mL) **vegetable oil**

14 oz (400 mL) **coconut milk**

1 cup (250 mL) **fish stock**, or chicken stock

2 strips **lemon rind**, about 2 inches × 1 inch (5 × 2.5 cm)

1 tbsp (15 mL) **Thai fish sauce**

3 cups (750 mL) **cooked rice**, white or brown

3 **green onions**, finely sliced, for garnish

2 **Thai red chili peppers**, finely sliced, for garnish

Wash and dry the fish fillets. Depending on the size, cut each fillet crosswise in half or in thirds so each piece measures about 3 inches (7.5 cm) in length. Refrigerate the fillets until ready to cook.

In a large skillet over medium heat, sauté the garlic, gingerroot, turmeric powder, and red chili peppers in the oil for one minute, stirring constantly. Add the coconut milk, fish stock, lemon rind, and Thai fish sauce. Bring to a boil.

Add the fish pieces to the coconut liquid, layering the fillets, if necessary. Return the liquid to the boil and gently simmer, uncovered, for 10 to 15 minutes, or until the fish is just cooked through.

To serve, spoon the cooked rice onto a large serving platter. Place the cooked fish on top of the rice and top with some sauce. Garnish with green onion and Thai red chili peppers.

Christmas Bell
Chile Pepper

50¢ each

Mild Heat

Chile Pepper

75¢ each or 3/$2.00

50,000-100,000 Scoville Units
(or 9 on a 1-10 scale)

Hot Hungarian
(aka hot banana)
Chile Pepper

$1.00 each

5,000-15,000 Scoville units

Jalapeno
Chile Pepper

50¢ each

Scoville units

Hot Portugal
Chile Pepper

$1.00 each

*Hot peppers grown by Grandora
Gardens, Saskatoon Farmers' Market.*

175

Steelhead Trout with Tomato-Cream Sauce

Saskatchewan is known for its beautiful lakes and excellent fishing. One fish that is very popular at fish shops across the province is farmed steelhead trout from Lake Diefenbaker. The lovely tomato-cream sauce is a beautiful complement to this tasty farm-raised fish.

SERVES 4 TO 6

1 large **steelhead trout** or salmon fillet, skin-on, about 1 ½ lbs (680 g)

2 tbsp (30 mL) **vegetable oil**

1 **yellow onion**, peeled and cut into thin wedges

1 **tomato**, diced

3 tbsp (45 mL) **white wine**

1 cup (250 mL) **35% cream**

1 handful **fresh dill fronds**, finely chopped

salt and **pepper**, to taste

Rinse the fish, and pat dry with a paper towel. With a sharp knife, cut the fillet crosswise into individual portions, each about 3 inches (7.5 cm) wide.

Heat a grill pan or skillet to medium-high. Add the oil and place the fillets, skin side down and flesh side up into the pan. Cook for about 4 to 5 minutes.

Turn the fillets over and season with salt and pepper. Cook for several more minutes and then remove the fish to a plate when just barely cooked. Loosely cover the fillets with a sheet of waxed paper and a tea towel. They will continue to cook for another minute after being removed from the pan.

Meanwhile, make the tomato-cream sauce using the same pan as the fish portions were cooked in. Sauté the onion wedges for about 1 minute. Add the tomato and sauté for another minute. Deglaze the pan with the white wine; then add the cream and dill. Season with salt and pepper. Bring to a boil. Reduce heat and simmer about 5 minutes, or until the sauce reduces slightly and thickens. Taste and adjust seasonings.

Spoon the sauce over the cooked fish.

Winter Bean Curry

This hearty vegetarian bean stew uses a variety of legumes—chickpeas, kidney beans, romano beans, and black beans. For a change of pace, substitute whole green lentils for some of the beans in this dish.

SERVES 6

1 cup (250 mL) chopped **onion**

4 cloves **garlic**, peeled and chopped

1 tbsp (15 mL) **vegetable oil**

2 large **potatoes**, chopped

1 large **carrot**, sliced

1 ¹/₂ tbsp (22 mL) **mild Indian-style curry paste**,* or 1 ¹/₂ tbsp (22 mL) curry powder

¹/₄ tsp (1 mL) **ground cumin**

¹/₂ tsp (2 mL) **mild curry powder**

¹/₂ tsp (2 mL) **ground cinnamon**

1 **bay leaf**

1 large or 2 medium **tomatoes**, peeled and chopped

4 cups (1 L) **chicken** or vegetable **stock**

4 cups (1 L) **cooked, mixed beans** (a combination of any of the following: chickpeas, kidney beans, romano beans, black beans, or whole lentils)

1 **apple**, peeled and coarsely chopped

2 tbsp (30 mL) **sweet mango chutney**

3 tsp (15 mL) **cornstarch**, whisked in a bowl with 1 tbsp (15 mL) **water**

6 **baby bok choy**, thick white ends removed (keep for another use) and the green leaves thinly sliced, or 6 oz (170 g) baby spinach, trimmed and thinly sliced

³/₄ tsp (3 mL) **kosher salt**

plain yogurt and additional **chutney**, for serving

In a Dutch oven or large pot, sauté the onion and garlic in the oil over medium heat for 1 to 2 minutes. Add the potatoes and carrot, and cook for about 5 minutes. Add the curry paste, cumin, curry powder, cinnamon, and bay leaf. Stir for 1 minute to toast the spices.

Add the chopped tomatoes and stock. Bring to a boil, scraping the bits off the bottom. Simmer uncovered, stirring occasionally, until the vegetables are soft, about 20 minutes.

Add the beans, apple, chutney, and cornstarch-water mixture, and simmer several minutes longer until the mixture has thickened slightly. Add the bok choy or spinach, and stir until wilted. Season with salt.

Spoon over cooked white or brown rice. Top with plain yogurt and additional chutney, if desired.

Indian-style curry paste is available in most supermarkets.

Thai Chicken Curry

Here's a delicious meal with international flair. This curry can easily be made in less than 30 minutes, making it a great weeknight dinner.

SERVES 4

Laying hens, Farmgate Food, Balgonie, SK.

1 lb (454 g) boneless, skinless **chicken breasts** or thighs

14 oz (400 mL) **coconut milk**

1 ½ tbsp (22 mL) **yellow curry paste**

1 tbsp (15 mL) **brown sugar**, or palm sugar, or muscovado sugar

1 tbsp (15 mL) **fish sauce**

1 **kaffir lime leaf**, very finely sliced, or about ¼ tsp (1 mL) finely grated lime zest

1 tbsp (15 mL) **peanut oil**

2 oz (56 g) halved **green beans** or broccoli florets

¼ cup (60 mL) firmly packed **fresh Thai basil leaves**, or cilantro, divided

¼ cup (60 mL) coarsely chopped **roasted, unsalted peanuts**

2 **Thai red chili peppers**, thinly sliced

Trim the chicken of any excess fat, and cut into bite-size pieces.

To prepare curry sauce, place the coconut milk, curry paste, sugar, fish sauce, and sliced lime leaf in wok or large frying pan. Bring to a boil. Reduce the heat and simmer for about 15 minutes or until the sauce reduces slightly; stir occasionally.

Meanwhile, heat the oil in separate large wok, or fry pan. Partially cook the chicken in batches until lightly browned. Drain on paper towel. Transfer the chicken to the wok with the curry sauce.

Add the beans or broccoli florets and half the Thai basil leaves to the curry sauce-chicken mixture. Simmer about 5 minutes or until the vegetables are tender and the chicken is cooked through.

Serve over cooked Jasmine rice. Garnish with the peanuts, sliced chili peppers, and the remaining basil.

Chicken Stir-Fry with Ginger and Chinese Cabbage

During the biting cold that blasts across the Prairies each winter, we eat more vegetables to stay healthy. This uplifting dish has the added benefit of plenty of fresh ginger and garlic to ward off any colds.

SERVES 4

1 lb (454 g) boneless, skinless **chicken thighs**, sliced into ¹/₂-inch (1.5 cm) thick slices

2 cloves **garlic**, peeled and sliced thinly

1 ¹/₂ inch (4 cm) piece of **fresh ginger**, peeled and sliced into thin matchsticks

2 **Thai red chili peppers**, finely chopped (or to taste)

4 cups (1 L) sliced **Chinese cabbage**, cut ¹/₂-inch (1.5 cm) wide

6 oz (170 g) **fresh green beans**, cut in half crosswise

1 tbsp (15 mL) **cornstarch**

1 tbsp (15 mL) **brown sugar**

2 tbsp (30 mL) **light soy sauce**

1 tbsp (15 mL) **rice wine vinegar**

1 tbsp (15 mL) **Asian sesame oil**

peanut oil, for sautéing

additional **light soy sauce**, for sautéing

2 **green onions**, finely sliced on the diagonal, for garnish

handful roughly chopped **fresh cilantro**, for garnish

Garlic bulbs.

Preheat a wok over high heat. Add about 2 tbsp (30 mL) peanut oil. The peanut oil will shimmer when it has reached the correct temperature. Add half the chicken thighs and brown on all sides, being careful not to fully cook the chicken. (Partially cooking the chicken ensures that the chicken will be moist and tender by the time the stir-fry is finished cooking.) Sprinkle with about 2 to 3 tsp (10 to 15 mL) soy sauce. Using a slotted spoon, remove the browned chicken to a plate and repeat the procedure with the remaining chicken.

In the same wok as you browned the chicken, add a bit more peanut oil (if necessary) and add the garlic, ginger, and chili peppers. Stir-fry the mixture quickly for about 1 minute, until fragrant. Add the Chinese cabbage and the green beans. Let the mixture cook for about 5 minutes, stirring occasionally.

Meanwhile, in a small bowl whisk together the cornstarch, brown sugar, soy sauce, rice wine vinegar, and sesame oil. Add it to the wok along with the browned chicken. Bring the sauce to a boil and cook another 5 minutes, until the chicken is fully cooked through and the sauce has thickened. Stir frequently.

Serve hot over cooked white rice. Garnish with a few green onions and cilantro.

Succulent Stuffed Chicken Breasts with Red Wine Sauce

I first served this dish at a wine-and-food-pairing cooking class. The stuffing and the red wine sauce have a richness that makes you believe you are dining in a first-class restaurant. This dish is lovely served with oven-roasted beets, and buttermilk mashed potatoes that have been seasoned with salt, pepper, and freshly grated nutmeg.

SERVES 4

Cambozola Cheese

Cambozola cheese is a semi-mild, soft-ripened, blue cheese made in Germany by the Champignon Company. It tastes like a cross between Camembert and Gorgonzola. It is available in most supermarkets. If you cannot find it, a very mild, creamy blue cheese would work well.

6 **pitted prunes**, finely chopped

¹/₈ cup (30 mL) **dried cranberries**, finely chopped

2 oz (56 g) **Cambozola cheese**, rind on, cut into small chunks

zest of half an orange

¹/₄ tsp (1 mL) cracked **black pepper**

kosher salt, to taste

4 boneless, skinless **chicken breasts**

2 tsp (10 mL) **Dijon mustard**

¹/₄ cup (60 mL) **unbleached, all-purpose flour**

¹/₄ tsp (1 mL) **kosher salt**

pepper

1 ¹/₂ tbsp (22 mL) **vegetable oil**

To make the filling, in a small bowl, combine the prunes, dried cranberries, cheese, orange zest, cracked black pepper, and salt. Mix with your fingers until the mixture resembles a very coarse paste. Refrigerate until ready to use.

Preheat oven to 400°F (200°C).

Butterfly each chicken breast by placing the flat smooth side of the chicken breast on a cutting board. With a sharp knife, position the blade horizontal to the work surface and slice the breast horizontally almost in two. Be careful to keep both sides the same thickness. Open the breast like a book.

Brush the inside of each breast with ¹/₂ tsp (2 mL) Dijon mustard. Divide the filling in four. Spread ¹/₄ of the filling on one side of each breast. Close, and tie each breast closed with butcher's string.

In a small bowl combine the flour, salt, and pepper; mix well. Dredge each breast in the flour mixture and set aside on a plate.

Heat a sauté pan to medium-high; add oil and brown each stuffed breast on all sides, about 5 to 8 minutes. Remove breasts to an ovenproof dish and place, uncovered, in the oven for 12 to 15 minutes to finish cooking. Remove the breasts to a plate and let rest, loosely covered with waxed paper and a tea towel, for 10 minutes. Meanwhile, prepare the Red Wine Sauce.

To serve, remove the string from each breast and slice each chicken breast into 5 to 6 slices. Spoon a small pool of sauce onto each plate and arrange the sliced chicken decoratively on top.

Serve with additional sauce.

RED WINE SAUCE

³/₄ cup (185 mL) **dry red wine**

1 ¹/₄ cups (300 mL) **homemade chicken stock**, or 1 can (10 oz/284 mL) chicken broth

juice of half an orange

6 tbsp (90 mL) *cold* **unsalted butter***

Using the same pan as the chicken was cooked in, deglaze pan with ¹/₂ cup (125 mL) red wine, scraping the dark bits off the bottom of the pan. Add the chicken broth, remaining red wine, and orange juice and let simmer until reduced by half. Whisk in the *cold* butter, 1 tbsp (15 mL) at a time (very important), whisking constantly until each piece of butter is completely melted before adding the next amount. Sauce will gradually thicken. Strain sauce through a sieve. Do not make the sauce ahead or it will break when reheated.

* Using cold butter is important, since room temperature butter will melt too quickly and the sauce won't thicken properly.

Mark Lane and his layer flock, Farmgate Food, Balgonie, SK.

Chicken with Dried Fruit and Port

This is a superb weekday meal with the flavours of the holiday season. If you wish to use red wine instead of the port, add 1 to 2 tbsp of honey to the sauce.

SERVES 4 TO 6

$^{1}/_{2}$ cup (125 mL) halved, **dried prunes**

$^{1}/_{4}$ cup (60 mL) **raisins**

$^{1}/_{4}$ cup (60 mL) **dried cranberries** or sliced dried apricots

$^{1}/_{2}$ cup (125 mL) **chicken stock**

1 tbsp (15 mL) **vegetable oil**

4 to 6 boneless, skinless **chicken breasts**

2 small **shallots**, finely diced

1 clove **garlic**, minced

1 tsp (5 mL) **ground cinnamon**

1 tsp (5 mL) **ground coriander**

1 cup (250 mL) **port** or sherry

$^{1}/_{4}$ cup (60 mL) **pine nuts**

salt and **pepper**, to taste

Preheat oven to 375°F (190°C).

Combine the prunes, raisins, and dried cranberries in a medium bowl. Heat the chicken stock to boiling and pour it over the fruit. Let stand for 1 hour.

In large skillet, add the oil and brown the chicken breasts over medium-high heat. Do not cook through. Transfer breasts to an oiled, shallow pan and bake, uncovered, for about 10 minutes, until just cooked through.

Meanwhile, in the same skillet, lightly sauté the shallots and garlic over medium-low heat, about 30 seconds. Add the cinnamon and coriander. Stir quickly and then deglaze the pan with the port. Add the pine nuts, soaked fruit, and chicken stock. Let simmer for about 10 minutes, until thick and syrupy.

Taste and adjust seasonings. Serve the sauce with the chicken.

Pan-Roasted Duck Breasts
with Savoury Lingonberry Sauce

This earthy dish shines with forest-grown lingonberries accented with honey and fresh thyme. Use chopped cranberries if you don't have access to lingonberries.

SERVES 6

6 **duck breasts**, about 5 oz (140 g) each, skin on

salt and **pepper**, to taste

Preheat oven to 450°F (235°C).

Preheat a cast-iron or heavy skillet on high heat. Score the skin of the duck breasts in a cross-hatch pattern, being careful not to slice through to the flesh. Season both sides with salt and pepper. Place the breasts, skin side down in the hot, ungreased skillet. Sear the skin about 5 minutes. Turn over and sear for another minute. (The breasts will splatter quite a bit.) Transfer the breasts to a parchment paper–lined cookie sheet. (Breasts can be prepared to this point and refrigerated until ready to cook. Bring to room temperature before continuing with recipe.)

Transfer the cookie sheet with the duck breasts to the oven and roast for 5 to 7 minutes, or until medium rare. Remove from the oven. Drape the breasts with a sheet of waxed paper and a tea towel. Let rest 10 minutes. Transfer to a cutting board; slice on the diagonal into slices of even thickness. Place on a serving platter and serve with Savoury Lingonberry Sauce.

Savoury Lingonberry Sauce

2 cups (500 mL) **dry red wine**

10 oz (284 mL) **chicken broth**

10 oz (284 mL) **beef broth**

5 sprigs **fresh thyme**

1 **bay leaf**

$^1/_2$ cup (125 mL) **lingonberries**, fresh or frozen, or chopped cranberries

2 tsp (10 mL) **all-purpose flour**

2 tsp (10 mL) soft **unsalted butter**

salt and **pepper**, to taste

2 tsp (10 mL) **honey**, or more, to taste

In a medium saucepan, combine the red wine, chicken broth, beef broth, thyme sprigs, and bay leaf. Bring to a boil, reduce heat, and simmer about 45 minutes, or until reduced to 1 $^1/_2$ cups (375 mL). Remove thyme sprigs and bay leaf. Add the lingonberries and cook until the berries start to pop.

In a small bowl, mix together the flour and the butter until completely emulsified and no lumps whatsoever remain. Add to the sauce and stir until the mixture has completely melted and the sauce slightly thickens. Add the honey. Taste the sauce and add more honey, if desired, being careful not to make the sauce too sweet. (The honey should just take the edge off the tartness of the berries.) Add salt and pepper, to taste. Remove from heat. Gently rewarm just before serving.

Apple-Lingonberry (or Cranberry) Strudel

Strudel is a classic dessert and easy to make with pre-made phyllo dough. This strudel is made with low-bush cranberries, also known as lingonberries. Cranberries are also excellent in this recipe. For variation, try the turnovers and cigars.

MAKES 2 STRUDELS, 16 SERVINGS

4 firm **apples** such as Prairie Sun, Gala, Spartan, or Granny Smith, or a mixture

²/₃ cup (160 mL) **pecan pieces**, toasted

1 ¹/₂ cups (375 mL) **lingonberries** or whole cranberries, frozen or fresh

finely grated **zest of 1 lemon**

²/₃ cup (160 mL) **granulated sugar**

4 tbsp (60 mL) **flour**, if using lingonberries, or 2 tbsp (30 mL) flour, if using cranberries

8 sheets **phyllo dough**, thawed in the refrigerator overnight

¹/₃ cup (80 mL) **vegetable oil** or melted butter

granulated sugar, for sprinkling

dry breadcrumbs, for sprinkling

Preheat oven to 375°F (190°C).

Peel and core apples and cut into ¹/₂-inch (1.5 cm) cubes. Coarsely chop toasted pecans. In a large bowl, combine the chopped apples, pecans, lingonberries, lemon zest, sugar, and flour. Toss well and set aside.

On a clean counter, lay out the phyllo dough and cover it with a barely damp tea towel. Peel off one sheet and lay it on a flat surface. Replace the damp tea towel on the stack of phyllo.

Brush the sheet of phyllo with oil or melted butter; sprinkle lightly with the sugar, and then the breadcrumbs. Continue with another 2 sheets, brushing each sheet with oil or butter, and sprinkling with sugar and breadcrumbs. End with a fourth sheet of phyllo.

Arrange half the fruit mixture along the long side of the phyllo about 2 inches (5 cm) from the edge of the bottom and sides of the dough. Starting at the edge nearest the filling, carefully begin to roll the phyllo over the filling. Tuck in the sides of the dough. Continue to roll up the strudel so the dough completely encases the filling. Tuck in any loose ends. Brush with oil or melted butter, sprinkle with more sugar.

Place the strudel seam side down on a parchment paper–lined cookie sheet. Cut 8 diagonal slits along the top to allow steam to escape and for easy cutting when you serve. Brush the top with oil or melted butter. Repeat the procedure for the other strudel.

Bake for 40 to 50 minutes, or until crisp and golden brown. If strudels begin to brown too much, set a sheet of aluminum foil on the top of the strudels.

Transfer to a wire rack to cool.

Just before serving, dust the top with icing sugar.

Turnovers or Cigars Variation

Take one sheet of phyllo, brush with the oil or melted butter and sprinkle with sugar and breadcrumbs. Top with another sheet of phyllo. Using a pizza cutter, cut the sheet into three equal strips along the long side of the dough. Place 1 tbsp (15 mL) of the filling on each strip. Roll up like a cigar, tucking in the ends, or fold into triangles folding as you would a flag. Brush with oil or melted butter and sprinkle with sugar. Bake at 375°F (190°C) for about 12 to 15 minutes.

Lentil Chocolate Cake

Lentils with dessert? A novel idea, and one that works wonders in this cake.

MAKES ONE 9 ¹/₂-INCH (24 CM) ROUND CAKE

1 ¹/₃ cups (330 mL) **unbleached all-purpose flour**

2 ¹/₂ tsp (12 mL) **baking powder**

¹/₄ tsp (1 mL) **baking soda**

¹/₂ tsp (2 mL) **kosher salt**

¹/₄ cup (60 mL) **unsalted butter**, room temperature

1 cup (250 mL) **granulated sugar**

1 tsp (5 mL) **pure vanilla extract**

2 **eggs**

2 oz (56 g) **dark chocolate**, 70% or 85%, melted and cooled

¹/₂ cup (125 mL) puréed **red lentils**, sieved (recipe follows)

1 cup (250 mL) **milk**

Leftover Lentils Tip

Leftover puréed lentils are a great addition to mashed potatoes or to dips such as hummus.

Preheat oven to 350°F (180°C). Prepare the puréed red lentils (see method below). Grease and flour a 9 ¹/₂-inch (24 cm) round cake tin. Set aside.

Scoop the flour gently into measuring cups. Level the top with the flat edge of a knife and transfer flour to a medium bowl. Add baking powder, baking soda, and salt. Set aside.

In a mixer bowl, beat the butter and sugar on medium speed until well combined. Continue mixing and add the vanilla extract. Then beat in the eggs, one at a time, beating well after each addition. On low speed, mix in the cooled melted chocolate and the cooled puréed lentils. Mix well, scraping down the sides of the bowl occasionally.

Add the dry ingredients alternately with the milk in three additions, beginning and ending with the dry ingredients.

Turn the batter into the prepared pan. Bake for 30 to 35 minutes, until a toothpick inserted into the centre comes out clean. Remove from the oven to a wire rack and let stand 10 minutes. Remove the cake from the tin and set the cake on a wire rack to cool completely. Frost as desired or dust lightly with a bit of sieved icing sugar and serve with a scoop of vanilla ice cream.

PURÉED RED LENTILS

1 ¹/₂ cups (375 mL) **water**

¹/₂ cup (125 mL) **split red lentils**

pinch **kosher salt**

In a small saucepan, bring the water, red lentils, and salt to a boil. Reduce heat and simmer, covered, about 30 minutes, stirring occasionally until the lentils have completely softened and are mushy. Mixture should be rather thick and the liquid evaporated. Remove from heat and transfer the mixture to a fine mesh sieve. Sieve the cooked lentils to remove any husks and partially cooked lentils that may remain. Let cool completely. Measure the required amount for the cake.

wheat
A PRAIRIE STAPLE

For well over a century, golden wheat fields, ripe for harvesting, have been symbolic of the prairies. Today, 80% of durum wheat and at least 50% of the entire wheat crop in Canada is grown by Saskatchewan farmers. The country's leader in cereal crop production, Saskatchewan supplies five percent of the world's total exported wheat. The numerous wheat classes are milled into a range of flours, each with a different protein and gluten level. Flour quality is determined by how suitable it is for baking bread: determinants include the dough's elasticity, the volume and crust of the baked loaf, and the quantity of water that's absorbed by the flour.

All-purpose flour is often a blend of hard and soft wheat flours. With a protein content of around 11%, it's a workhorse suitable for being mixed, stretched, and kneaded into hearty yeast breads, and for being delicately handled to make the flakiest pastry. The recipes presented in this cookbook were developed using unbleached, all-purpose flour. All-purpose flour is pre-sifted, so give it a good stir to fluff and aerate it before measuring.

Bread flour is milled from Canada Western Hard Spring wheat and has a high protein content, between 12.5% and 14%. It's used by professional bakers, since the high gluten content works to form an elastic web when kneaded. This elasticity means that the dough is strong enough to withstand long periods of rising and stretching; yet, it still bakes into a tender, fine-textured bread. Use it for doughs that have to be well worked, such as yeast breads, puff pastry, and Danish pastry.

Cake and pastry flour is milled from Canada Western Soft White Spring wheat and has a low protein content, between 7% and 8%. This flour gives a light and delicate crumb to baking powder biscuits and cakes, particularly angel food cakes and chiffon cakes. It's ideal to create a light and flaky pie crust. Because it clumps when left standing, always sift cake and pastry flour before using.

Semolina flour is made from Canada Western Amber durum wheat and is fairly coarse. If you love to make pasta, this flour is ideal for creating a strong pasta. It's often found in specialty stores.

Whole wheat flour has a nutty flavour because the whole grain is milled. The bran and the germ give the flour its darker, coarser appearance. It adds a somewhat coarse texture to baked goods.

Canada's high-quality flour is the best in the world. Bakers around the globe love it for its exceptional taste, aroma, texture, quality, and appearance. Canadian flour travels to international kitchens to be made into German rye, Danish pastry, French puff pastry, and the finest Italian pasta. How lucky we are that this desirable ingredient is a staple in our own kitchens and pantries.

TOP LEFT: *A field of wheat just weeks from harvest. Stoney Beach, SK.*

TOP RIGHT: *Durum wheat.*

Bread Pudding with Brandied Fruit

Some foods just give us a warm fuzzy feeling inside. Bread pudding is one of them. It reminds me of my childhood, when bread pudding was still very much a common dessert. This recipe was developed using dinner rolls made at Arm River Hutterite Colony, located just outside Lumsden, Saskatchewan. Meals at Lydia and Dave's home were always generous. After a grand supper and a very pleasant evening, they would send Michael and me home with a handsome supply of delicious dinner rolls the colony women had baked that morning. Often, there were more rolls than we could eat before they started to go stale. I hated to waste them, so I developed this decadent version of bread pudding. The fresh and dried fruit, the orange zest, and the splash of brandy elevate it more than a step above the modest bread pudding of my childhood.

SERVES 6 TO 8

2 ¼ cups (560 mL) **stale dinner rolls**, or stale white bread, trimmed of crusts and cubed

½ cup (125 mL) chopped **dried apricots**

¼ cup (60 mL) **brandy**

1 cup (250 mL) **fresh plums**
or nectarines (about 2 to 3 large), skin-on, pitted and diced

zest of 1 orange, finely grated

2 **eggs**

⅓ cup (80 mL) **granulated sugar**

1 ½ tsp (7 mL) **pure vanilla extract**

¾ cup (185 mL) cold **milk**

¼ cup (60 mL) cold **35% cream**

1 tbsp (15 mL) **butter**, melted

freshly grated **nutmeg**

Dean Kreutzer at Over the Hill Orchards in Lumsden, SK, is working to breed a hardy apricot that will survive the cold prairie winters.

In a glass measuring cup, warm the brandy in the microwave, about 30 seconds, and combine it with the chopped apricots. Let stand 30 minutes. Strain the apricots. Reserve the brandy.

Preheat oven to 350°F (180°C).

In large bowl, combine the bread, apricots, diced plums, and finely grated orange zest. Mix well. Transfer to a buttered 6-cup (1.5 L) soufflé or casserole dish.

In a medium bowl, whisk the eggs by hand until frothy and slightly thickened, about 1 minute. Add the sugar and whisk another minute. Add the vanilla. Whisk in the milk, cream, and melted butter. Add the reserved brandy. Pour the milk-brandy mixture over the bread and fruit. Let it stand for 20 minutes to absorb the liquid.

Top with freshly grated nutmeg.

Bake uncovered for 50 minutes, or until a knife inserted into the centre comes out clean. Cool slightly before serving.

Cranberry Coconut-Cream Torte

This show-stopper cake will definitely add "wow" to your Christmas dinner. The cranberry filling needs to be made ahead to allow time for it to chill completely, which makes this cake ideal for holiday entertaining. You can bake the cake ahead of time, too, then assemble it on the day of your party.

SERVES 10 TO 12

1 ¹/₂ cups (375 mL) **unbleached all-purpose flour**

2 ¹/₂ tsp (12 mL) **baking powder**

¹/₂ tsp (2 mL) **kosher salt**

¹/₃ cup (80 mL) **unsalted butter**

1 cup (250 mL) **granulated sugar**

¹/₄ tsp (1 mL) **pure almond extract**

2 large **eggs**

1 cup (250 mL) **coconut milk**

1 cup (250 mL) **shredded coconut**, sweetened or unsweetened

whole cranberries for garnish

CAKE: Preheat oven to 350°F (180°C).

Grease and line with parchment paper one 8 ¹/₂-inch or 9 ¹/₂-inch (21.5 or 24 cm) round springform pan.

Scoop the flour gently into the measuring cups. Level the top with the flat edge of a knife. Transfer the flour to a medium bowl and add the baking powder and salt. Stir to combine. Set aside.

In a large mixer bowl fitted with a paddle, cream the butter and sugar together until light. Add the almond flavouring. Add the eggs one a time, beating well after each addition.

Slowly fold in one-third of the dry ingredients until just mixed. Add half the coconut milk, stirring just to combine. Add another third of the dry ingredients, then the coconut milk, and end with the dry ingredients. Transfer the batter to the prepared springform pan.

Bake for 35 to 40 minutes until the cake just starts to pull away from the sides of the pan and the centre springs back when touched. Let the cake cool in the pan for 10 minutes before removing to a wire rack to cool completely.

ASSEMBLY: With a large serrated knife, cut the cake into two layers. Place the bottom layer, cut side up, on a cake plate. Spread the layer with the cooled Cranberry Filling. Top with the second layer, cut side down.

Spread the Cream Frosting on the top and sides of the cake. Sprinkle top and sides of cake with shredded coconut. Decorate with a few whole cranberries.

CRANBERRY FILLING

1 ½ cups (375 mL) **whole cranberries**, frozen or fresh

½ cup (125 mL) **liquid honey**

⅓ cup (80 mL) **orange marmalade**

Combine the whole cranberries, honey, and orange marmalade in a medium saucepan. Bring to a boil and then simmer until cranberries pop and the mixture thickens. Cool completely in the refrigerator.

CREAM FROSTING

1 ½ cups (375 mL) **35% cream**

2 tbsp (30 mL) **icing sugar**

½ tsp (2 mL) **pure vanilla extract**

Whip the cream to very soft peaks. Add the icing sugar and vanilla extract and beat until stiff peaks form.

Lingonberry Cheesecake
with Sweet Lingonberry Sauce

This is a "died-and-gone-to-heaven" cheesecake. Lingonberries grow in the boreal forest. They are ripe for picking in the fall and can be picked throughout the winter months. You can substitute chopped cranberries and get equally delicious results.

SERVES 12

CRUST

³/₄ cup (185 mL) **graham cracker crumbs**

¹/₂ cup (125 mL) chopped **pecan pieces**

¹/₄ cup (60 mL) **granulated sugar**

¹/₄ cup (60 mL) **melted butter**

Preheat oven to 375°F (190°C).

Place the graham cracker crumbs, pecan pieces, and sugar into a food processor bowl. Process about 30 seconds until the nuts are very finely chopped. Add the melted butter and process another 20 seconds. Transfer the mixture to a 9-inch (23 cm) springform pan. Pat gently to form a crust on the bottom of the pan. Bake for 8 minutes. Remove from the oven.

Clean the food processor bowl and blade.

Decrease the oven temperature to 350°F (180°C).

FILLING

12 oz (340 g) **regular cream cheese**, room temperature

³/₄ cup (185 mL) **granulated sugar**

pinch **kosher salt**

finely grated **zest of half a lemon**

¹/₂ tsp (2 mL) **pure vanilla extract**

2 **eggs**

¹/₂ cup (125 mL) **whole lingonberries**, fresh or frozen, or coarsely chopped cranberries

Cut the cream cheese into large cubes. Add the cubes to the food processor bowl and process until completely smooth, scraping the sides of the bowl often. Add the sugar and process another 10 to 15 seconds. Add the salt, lemon zest, and vanilla. Process several seconds until combined. Add the eggs one at a time. Mix well. Transfer the mixture to a medium bowl and stir in whole lingonberries or chopped cranberries. Transfer the batter to the springform pan with the baked crust.

Bake 25 to 30 minutes at 350°F (180°C) until centre is slightly firm. Remove from oven.

Increase the oven temperature to 450°F (235°C).

¹/₂ cup (125 mL) **plain 2% yogurt**

¹/₂ cup (125 mL) **sour cream**

2 tbsp (30 mL) **granulated sugar**

¹/₄ tsp (1 mL) **almond extract**

In a small bowl, mix together the yogurt, sour cream, sugar, and almond extract. Gently spread the mixture over the hot cheesecake. Return the cheesecake to the oven and bake for another 5 minutes at 450°F (235°C). Remove from the oven to cool completely. Refrigerate until firm.

To serve, run a clean knife around the edge of the cheesecake. Remove the sides of the pan. Cut a wedge of cheesecake and transfer to a dessert plate. Top with the cold Sweet Lingonberry Sauce.

Sweet Lingonberry Sauce

2 cups (500 mL) **lingonberries**, fresh or frozen, or halved cranberries

1 cup (250 mL) cold **water**

³/₄ cup (185 mL) **granulated sugar**

1 tbsp *plus* 1 tsp (20 mL) **cornstarch**

finely grated **zest of half a lemon**

In a small saucepan, combine the lingonberries, cold water, sugar, and cornstarch. Bring to a boil and cook until the berries pop and mixture slightly thickens. Add the zest of half a lemon. Cool completely. (The mixture will thicken as it cools.)

Lingonberries, Kristi Lake, SK.

Lingonberry (or Cranberry) Lemon Loaf

This loaf is fabulous with a cup of tea. It stays moist for a week.

MAKES ONE 9- × 5-INCH (2 L) LOAF

2 cups (500 mL) **unbleached all-purpose flour**

1/2 tsp (2 mL) **baking powder**

1/4 tsp (1 mL) **baking soda**

1/4 tsp (1 mL) **kosher salt**

1 1/2 cups (375 mL) **granulated sugar**

2 **eggs**

3/4 cup (185 mL) **melted butter**

1 tsp (5 mL) **pure vanilla extract**

3/4 cup (185 mL) **plain yogurt**

1/2 cup (125 mL) **milk**

finely grated **zest of 1 lemon**

1 cup (250 mL) **whole lingonberries**, or coarsely chopped cranberries, fresh or frozen

4 tbsp (60 mL) **fresh lemon juice**

1/3 cup (80 mL) **granulated sugar**

Lingonberries, Kristi Lake, SK.

Preheat oven to 325°F (165°C). Grease the loaf pan and line the bottom with parchment or waxed paper.

In a large bowl, combine the unbleached all-purpose flour, baking powder, baking soda, salt, and sugar.

In a medium bowl, whisk the eggs, melted butter, vanilla extract, plain yogurt, milk, and lemon zest until well combined. The mixture may curdle slightly.

Add the milk mixture to the flour mixture and stir until almost mixed. Fold in the whole lingonberries or the chopped cranberries. Transfer the mixture to the greased loaf pan. Bake for 70 to 80 minutes. Remove from the oven and let rest for 10 minutes.

Meanwhile, in a glass measuring cup, stir the lemon juice with the sugar. Heat in the microwave for about 20 to 30 seconds. Stir until the sugar has dissolved.

Once the loaf has cooled for 10 minutes, prick the top of the loaf all over with a toothpick or a bamboo skewer. Slowly pour the lemon syrup over the top of the loaf and let the loaf stand for several hours to completely absorb the liquid. Remove the loaf from the pan and slice.

Rugelach

This cookie makes an appearance in our household once a year at Chanukah and Christmas. Studded with cinnamon, nuts, and apricot jam, it's the perfect festive cookie.

MAKES 48 COOKIES

1 cup (250 mL) **unsalted butter**, room temperature

8 oz (226 g) **regular cream cheese**, softened

¹/₂ tsp (2 mL) **kosher salt**

2 ¹/₂ cups (625 mL) **unbleached all-purpose flour**

1 **egg**

1 tsp (5 mL) **water**

about ¹/₂ cup (125 mL) **granulated sugar**, for dipping

8 tbsp (120 mL) good quality **apricot jam**, divided

6 tsp (30 mL) **granulated sugar**, divided

5 tsp (25 mL) **ground cinnamon**, divided

12 tbsp (180 mL) **dried currants** (not raisins), divided

12 tbsp (180 mL) **chopped walnuts**, or pecans, divided

Preheat oven to 350°F (180°C). Line cookie sheets with parchment paper.

Beat the butter and cream cheese until light and well blended. Add the salt and flour and mix until the dough comes together. Divide the dough into four equal portions. Form each into a round ball and flatten slightly. Wrap in plastic wrap or waxed paper and chill one to two hours or freeze about 10 minutes.

In a small bowl, whisk together the egg and water. Set aside. In another small bowl, put about ¹/₂ cup (125 mL) granulated sugar. Set aside.

Roll one piece of dough into an 11-inch (28 cm) circle. Spread with 2 tbsp (30 mL) jam, then sprinkle with 1 ¹/₂ tsp (7 mL) sugar, 1 ¹/₄ tsp (6 mL) cinnamon, and 3 tbsp (45 mL) each currants and walnuts.

With the long edge of the rolling pin, gently press the nuts and currants into the filling. Using a pizza cutter, cut the circle into 12 equal wedges. Roll up each wedge, starting with the wide end, to make a small crescent.

Brush the top of each crescent with beaten egg and then dip the top into the granulated sugar. Set the crescents sugar side up on the cookie sheet.

Bake about 25 minutes, until golden. Immediately transfer the cookies to a wire rack to cool completely.

Before continuing with the next batch, scrape off the cookie sheet and wipe the pizza cutter and work surface clean.

Hamantaschen

Every Jewish child grows up eating this cookie at Purim, a festival that is celebrated one month before Easter. This recipe is my own variation, with a non-traditional cream-cheese dough and my twist on a dried uncooked fruit filling that I received from my son Aidan's first Montessori teacher, Erin Gailor—it is divine.

MAKES ABOUT 4 DOZEN

CREAM CHEESE DOUGH

1 cup (250 mL) **unsalted butter**, room temperature

8 oz (226 g) **regular cream cheese**, room temperature

$^1/_2$ tsp (2 mL) **kosher salt**

2 $^1/_2$ cups (625 mL) **unbleached all-purpose flour**

$^1/_2$ cup (125 mL) **icing sugar**

DRIED FRUIT FILLING

13 oz (370 g) **pitted prunes**

$^3/_4$ cup (185 mL) **raisins**

$^3/_4$ cup (185 mL) **dried cranberries**, or dried sour cherries

1 whole **orange**, rind on, washed, seeds removed, and roughly chopped into pieces

2 tbsp (30 mL) **granulated sugar**

1 **egg**

1 tsp (5 mL) **water**

$^1/_4$ cup (60 mL) **granulated sugar**

Preheat oven to 350°F (180°C). Line two cookie sheets with parchment paper.

DOUGH: In a processor bowl fitted with a metal blade, combine the butter, cream cheese, salt, flour, and icing sugar. Process until the mixture becomes a ball. Remove and divide the dough into four equal portions. Pat each portion into a disc and wrap in waxed paper. Refrigerate about 1 hour. Clean the food processor bowl.

FILLING: In a clean food processor bowl fitted with a metal blade, mix half the prunes, half the raisins, half the cranberries, half the orange pieces, and 1 tbsp (15 mL) sugar. Process to a rough paste. Remove mixture to a bowl. Repeat with remaining ingredients.

TO MAKE THE COOKIES: In a small bowl, whisk together the egg and the water. Set aside.
    Roll out the dough on a floured surface to $^1/_8$-inch (3 mm) thickness. Cut the dough, using a metal cookie cutter or a glass, into 2-inch (5 cm) circles. Brush the edges of each circle with beaten egg. Place about 1 tsp (5 mL) of the fruit mixture in the centre of the circle. Pinch edges together to form a triangle with an open centre (it will look like a tricorn hat). Brush the pastry with the beaten egg and sprinkle with some of the granulated sugar. Bake for about 25 minutes, or until lightly brown on the outside. Remove to a wire rack to cool.

Cranberry-Ginger Chutney

This chutney is a fabulous addition to any Christmas dinner. Try it as a topping for soft cheeses such as Brie and Camembert. Be sure to use dried blueberries (available from health food stores)—fresh or frozen blueberries do not work in this recipe. Make the chutney one day ahead to give the blueberries time to reconstitute.

MAKES ABOUT 2 ¹/₂ CUPS (625 ML)

12 oz (340 g) **whole cranberries**, fresh or frozen

¹/₂ cup (125 mL) **dried blueberries**

¹/₄ cup (60 mL) **crystalized ginger**, cut into small pieces

³/₄ cup (185 mL) **granulated sugar**

¹/₄ cup (60 mL) **liquid honey**

¹/₂ cup (125 mL) **port**

¹/₂ cup (125 mL) **orange juice**

finely grated **zest of 1 orange**

finely grated **zest of 1 lemon**

In a medium pot, combine the cranberries, dried blueberries, crystalized ginger, sugar, honey, port, and orange juice. Bring to a boil and cook until the cranberries have popped and the mixture starts to thicken. Remove from heat and add the orange and lemon zest. Cool overnight in the refrigerator.

Liquid Gold Carrot Jam

I worked as an editor and food stylist on a cookbook called *Discover Carrots* by Helen Kudzin. One of my favourite discoveries in that cookbook was this absolutely delicious jam, which I shared with CBC-Radio Saskatchewan's audience during one of their Christmas specials. Within hours, there was a run on fresh ginger. Listeners e-mailed to tell me that they couldn't find ginger anywhere. This recipe doesn't use pectin. If you prefer a jam that is not as soft, boil it a little longer until more of the liquid has evaporated.

MAKES 4 ONE-PINT JARS

2 cups (500 mL) finely grated, peeled **carrots**

1 can (19 oz/540 mL) **crushed pineapple**, undrained

2 1/2 cups (625 mL) **granulated sugar**

2 tbsp (30 mL) coarsely grated, peeled, **fresh gingerroot**

5 tsp (25 mL) finely grated **lemon zest**, about 2 lemons

3 tbsp (45 mL) freshly squeezed **lemon juice**

Place the grated carrots, undrained crushed pineapple, and sugar into a large saucepan and stir to mix thoroughly. Stir the grated gingerroot and lemon zest into the carrot mixture. Bring to a boil over medium-high heat. Immediately reduce the heat and simmer 25 to 30 minutes, stirring occasionally until the mixture is thick and the pineapple is translucent.

Remove the carrot mixture from the heat and stir in the lemon juice.

Pour the jam into prepared containers. Cool completely and cover.

Store in the refrigerator or freeze. This jam will keep for four weeks in the refrigerator, but it won't last that long—it is that good!

The liquid in the jam will firm up as it cools, but it is slightly softer in texture than traditional jam. Stir before using.

Acknowledgements

Saskatchewan is rich in all manner of food producers, pickers of wild products, nature experts, shopkeepers, chefs, and local food lovers. All are passionate about growing and eating local food, and each enthusiastically embraced my idea of writing a Saskatchewan cookbook. They willingly gave of their time and knowledge, and opened their world to give me a glimpse of their lives, to learn about their passion, and to take photos. To each of them I am humbly grateful.

In particular, I'd like to thank Dean and Sylvia Kreutzer at Over the Hill Orchards; Henry Vanderleest at Very Berry Farm; David and Hazel Tanner at Pure T Organics, Ray and Marianne Aspinall at Daybreak-Scheresky Mill; Cheryl and Warren Dodds at Lumsden Sheep; Mark and Lynn Lane at Farmgate Food; Michelle Frischholz at Zee-Bee Honey; Jeff Fritzsche at Butcher Boy (Park St.) in Regina; Marin Waddell and James Holtom at SalayView Farms; bee producer Scott Lipsit; Chris Buhler at Floating Gardens; Tony Kustiak at K5 Market; Terry Helary at Northern Lights Foods; Rob Schulz at G & S Marina Outfitters; fishing biologists and outdoor educators Jeff and Jason Matity; Kim Sakundiak and Wayne Gienow at Lincoln Gardens; Brian Ross at Ross L-7 Ranch; Jack and Kim Hextall at Hextall Livestock; flax farmers Wayne and Mary Hart; fishing enthusiast Patrick Chernych; wild mushroom experts Gerry Ivanochko and Dave Kowalishen; bird and nature expert Carman Dodge; Gord Schroeder at Saskatchewan Sheep Development Board; Terry Kremeniuk at the Canadian Bison Association; Bob Bors and Rick Sawatzky at the University of Saskatchewan Fruit Program; Glen Sweetman and Mitchell Japp at the Saskatchewan Ministry of Agriculture; and Dr. Brian and Indra Datta.

I'd especially like to thank: Carl Worth at CTV for the opportunity to bring viewers into my *Wheatland Café* kitchen and to share my recipes; and of course, to my camera crew and co-hosts J.C. Garden and Angel Blair for loving every mouthful; my proofreader and mother-in-law, Ruth Katz, for scrupulously dotting every "i" and crossing every "t" and for asking so many astute questions. Working with you, Ima, was a joy! Cookbook author and dear friend Gay Cook, for her shoulder to lean on, for her invaluable culinary advice, and for her unyielding encouragement; my recipe testers, Jane Owen, Joan Zook, and Bonnie Fowler for their patience as I inundated them with recipes, and for their palates and valuable feedback; my photography teacher, Lori Maxim, for her photographic expertise and for being a solid supporter of my work, and her student Tamara Klein, who took the photo of me that appears on the inside back flap. And Shaq Tcherni, just because.

Special thanks to my team at the Canadian Plains Research Center: Deborah Rush, Duncan Campbell, and Donna Grant, who were passionate about this work since I presented it to them in the fall of 2010. Their thoughtful ideas and enthusiasm for Saskatchewan-grown food helped craft this book into a valuable addition to the history of Saskatchewan food and Canadian cuisine.

And finally, nothing would be possible without the support of my beloved sons, Aidan and Benjamin, and my husband Michael. Their unwavering encouragement and support for my work and for this cookbook mean more to me than anyone will know.

Sources

Agriculture and Agri-Food Canada. *Lentils: Situation and Outlook. Market Outlook Report*, Vol. 2 No. 2 (August 3, 2010). www.agr.gc.ca/gaod-dco

Archibold, O.W. *Wild Rice in Saskatchewan: Agricultural Development in Harmony with Nature, A Reference Manual.* Sasktchewan Education, Training and Employment and Saskatchewan Agriculture and Food.

Canadian Bison. www.canadianbison.ca

Daley, Regan. *In the Sweet Kitchen: The Definitive Guide to the Baker's Pantry.* Random House Canada, 2000.

The Encyclopedia of Saskatchewan (on-line). www.esask.uregina.ca

Government of Saskatchewan and Saskatchewan Ministry of Agriculture. www.agriculture.gov.sk.ca

Ivanochko, Gerry. *Saskatchewan NTFP Report.* La Ronge, SK: Saskatchewan Agriculture and Food, 2007.

Kowalishen, David D. Morels 101 [self-published booklet], 2004.

Kuo, Michael. *Morels.* University of Michigan Press, 2005.

Saskatchewan Pulse Growers. www.saskpulse.com

Saskatchewan Watershed Authority. *Fish Species of Saskatchewan.*

Yadav, Shyam, David McNeil, and Philip C. Stevenson. *Lentil: An Ancient Crop for Modern Times.* Springer, 2007.

index

Early Praise for *Taste*...

This stunning book is a treasure trove of the tastes and temptations that the prairie soil brings to life each season. The colours are beyond the traditional prairie palette, the recipes are a feast for the senses and you will discover many things about our homeland. This compendium is an inspiration to plant your garden, take a walk through the forests that cling to the sides of our highways, or take to the kitchen with a new enthusiasm!

It's a reflection of our new spirit—moving beyond the comfort zone of what we think of as traditional prairie fare.

Food for the Saskatchewan soul indeed!!

—the Honourable PAMELA WALLIN, Senator, Saskatchewan

Taste: Seasonal Dishes from a Prairie Table is an eye-opening treasury of distinctly western Canadian recipes. Each dish is lovingly drawn from the homegrown ingredients of the Prairie larder.

—KARL WELLS, food columnist, *The Telegram*, St. John's

CJ captures the richness and beauty of Saskatchewan in her words and photos. This is a beautiful book, not just for its terrific recipes but for its tribute to the people and the land around us. It made this Prairie boy hungry and brought a tear to my eye at the same time.

—JOHN GILCHRIST, Calgary food writer

Take a bumper harvest of lucid prairie recipes, fold them around personal anecdotes, local details and food lore, then garnish generously with CJ's own glorious photographs: a fascinating portrait of Saskatchewan's foodways emerges. What a delicious introduction to Canada's heartland!

—JAMES CHATTO, Toronto food writer